MW00695486

"As a film producer, I have tried many y
memoir] off the ground and have come
ecutives responded that there was 'no wa, ...
programmers feared this was too little known an event to draw an audience.
More the reason why Ms. Kuhn's story must be included in the Holocaust Survivor's Memoirs Project. It is a piece of history that unless documented now, will
go down as little more than a footnote in history...[The historical Rosenstrasse
Protest] started with just a few women demanding that their family members
be released, and turned into a protest of thousands...the <u>only</u> protest ever in
Nazi Germany. Fearing anti-Nazi sentiment (the women protesting were Aryan
women married to Jewish men), the Nazis backed down and released the men
and children. Which makes one think: *What if others had had the courage and
conviction to speak out against the Nazis?* Rita's mother was one of the bold
women who stood up to Hitler...and won."

—BETH GROSSBARD, EXECUTIVE PRODUCER,
CRAIG ANDERSON PRODUCTIONS

"This is an extraordinary memoir. It is a work of high intelligence and deep feeling. Both the general reader and the specialized scholars will gain much from it."

—SAMUEL HABER, PROFESSOR OF HISTORY, EMERITUS,
UNIVERSITY OF CALIFORNIA, BERKELEY

"The narrator tells a deeply moving and wrenching story of her girlhood in Nazi
Berlin. She speaks with power and eloquence for all those abruptly silenced
voices she once knew and loved. It is an important story with great narrative
strength to lead us through tragic episodes to a final triumph against all odds."

—BAYARD W. ALLMOND, M.D. F.A.A.P., BEHAVIORAL PEDIATRICIAN,
FORMER DIRECTOR OF THE CHILD UNIT, UCSF

"Rita makes the readers feel that they are there with her experiencing the horror firsthand. She imparts the sense of immediacy which compels the reader to
continue on to the end of her story. As a Holocaust educator, this is essential
reading for students to understand the lamentable consequences of hatred of
'the other.' "

—SHEILA JUDENFREUND, TEACHER IN A PROGRAM FOR GIFTED CHILDREN
AND HEBREW SCHOOL PRINCIPAL

"Rita Kuhn's memoir vividly evokes the experience of a child in Nazi Berlin. This important narrative compels the reader to relive a significant period in history."

—VIDA LEHMAN, TEACHER

"This memoir gives an unforgettable account of World War II, told by a Jewish survivor, Rita Kuhn, who was not afraid to tell her story so that the world would not forget what happened."

—ROSE GINSBURG, BERKELEY, CA

"In this simple yet profound narrative, Rita Kuhn brings us into the world of Hitler's Berlin and her response to it. In a remarkably clear and consistent style of writing, she takes the reader through years of unthinkable challenges, reaffirming her love of family and friends, and the resilience of her Jewish faith."

—RUTH WITTMAN, MANAGING EDITOR, PUSHCART PRIZE

BROKEN GLASS, BROKEN LIVES

A Jewish Girl's Survival Story
in Berlin, 1933-1945

RITA J. KUHN

Published by Barany Publishing,
771 Kingston Ave., #108
Piedmont, CA 94611.

Cover design and layout by Ezra Barany.

ISBN-13: 978-0-9832960-6-5
ISBN-10: 0-9832960-6-5

Printed in the U.S.A.

This book is available at special quantity discounts for bulk purchases. For details, and to request speaking
engagements with Rita J. Kuhn, please contact: Barany Publishing, 771 Kingston Ave., #108, Piedmont, CA
94611
BaranyPublishing.com

In loving memory to my parents:
Fritz and Frieda Kuhn,
who lived the past with me;
to my children:
Kenneth, Rachel, Sarah, Ruth,
who give me the courage to face it;
and to my grandchildren:
Ilya, Benjamin, Ariana, Irit, Ilse,
the next generation who will remember.

Contents

Foreword

After trying in vain to transcribe a tape-recorded interview with one Lotte Müller, a growly spitfire Berliner who had been imprisoned in Ravensbrück Concentration Camp for being a Communist, I needed help. The interview itself in Frau Müller's East Berlin apartment had been difficult, my hard-won Hochdeutsch no match for her Berlinerisch; I was never sure what she answered to my questions.

Through some avenue now forgotten, I approached the Holocaust Center of Northern California in San Francisco, whose late leader, Lani Silver, urged me to place a query in the Center's newsletter. I did. The question: can anyone who understands Berlin dialect help me?

Rita Kuhn of Fulton Street, Berkeley, formerly of Sybelstrasse, Berlin, answered *ja*.

Ja!

The result, encompassing many, many hand-written pages in pencil on a lined yellow notepad, not to mention many, many hours playing back the tape recordings was invaluable, perhaps even a gift. (Rita, did you accept payment for this work?) At some point in the long labor (Lotte was not one to spare words), Rita Kuhn said perhaps I would like to hear her own story.

Well, I thought, hesitating. Hmm. The book I was writing focused on the largely unexplained category of non-Jewish women during the Third Reich. I knew by now that Rita was a *"Geltungsjüdin,"* (a Nazi definition meaning a Jew by Law). I had basically finished interviewing; Rita was younger than the women I had interviewed, a small child when the Nazis came to power. As someone especially interested in moral decisions, as in who would risk what for whom, I wondered what could a child really know and decide?

By now, however, Rita and I were amiably connected via the emerging character of Lotte, and I certainly was in her debt. Okay, I said. More dutifully than enthusiastically, my tape-recorder at the ready, I made my way across San Francisco Bay to Rita's Berkeley apartment.

That was nearly a quarter century ago.

The fact that I stopped by there just yesterday tells What Happened Next. Rita's story was so complex and compelling, I made it the last chapter in my book. When readers get to her, past *Hausfrau*, onlookers, war widows, Nazi party members, a rescuer, a guard, a resister, a trio of farm women, a countess, a librarian, her voice acts as a truth filter to the tales that preceded hers. The complexity in Rita's account, then and now, is that her mother had been, in Nazi terminology, a polluter of her "Aryan" race by converting to Judaism and marriage to her Jewish father. A minor Nazi official once responded to her complaint about reduced food rations for Jews with, "Why did you whore with a Jew?" The complexity includes Rita's twofer. We receive not only extraordinary observations of the comically bizarre from her Nazi-dominated childhood and adolescence, but the fruits of a worldly, academically-enhanced education. Frau Doctor Kuhn, indeed!

Together these views, from a terrified child and a contemplative adult delineate the measure of a horror through a most precise prism.

We are fortunate to have *Broken Glass, Broken Lives*, a fuller and richer picture than I was privy to years ago. Readers be forewarned, however. In Rita Kuhn's world view, everyone, including Germans, is an individual.

—ALISON OWINGS
Author of *Frauen: German women recall the Third Reich.*

BROKEN GLASS, BROKEN LIVES

A Jewish Girl's Survival Story in Berlin, 1933-1945

Chapter 1

Into the Silence

Fair seed-time had my soul, and I grew up
Fostered alike by beauty and by fear.
—WORDSWORTH, "*The Prelude*"

The early morning light broke through the lace curtain of our narrow bedroom window. A few rays of sunlight resting on the floor and on the furniture told me that it was time to get up. Standing up in my crib, I glanced around the room and, looking across to my parents' bed, saw my father's head hidden partly by the bed covers. To the left side of the bed, a large, brown armoire dominated the room and I knew it was a hiding place for my parents' clothes. On the opposite wall was a door leading to the rest of the apartment, which belonged to my grandparents whom I was beginning to know by the names of "Opa," and "Oma." My mother had disappeared just moments ago through that door and left my father sleeping soundly in their bed.

As the firstborn, not yet two years old, I still had the unrivaled attention of my parents and was the sole ruler over their time and energy. Half that claim to their servitude I would have to relinquish to my brother, Hans, after his birth in 1930. But on that morning, feeling wide awake and no longer interested in the toys my mother had tossed into the crib, I wanted to assert that claim and tried to rouse my father from his huge feather pillow. He seemed oblivious to the sounds I made and his breathing continued audibly and evenly. I began to rattle the bars of my crib, now my prison, to have my father take me into bed with him and throw me into the billowing feather quilts that looked to me like mountains of whipped cream.

There was no response from the immobile figure in the bed. Some urge deep inside me was trying to tell me, though I had no words for it, that if obstacles stand in the way between me and my desire, I must try to climb over them. And so I tried; stretching and straining myself to full length until, standing on my toes, I bent over the bars of my crib in an effort to leave it and join the larger world. I must have been near to accomplishing my purpose because, all of a sudden, I saw my father, clad in a knee-length nightgown, push the covers aside and rush towards me. I felt his arms lift me out of the crib and put me gently on the floor.

Ah, the world was mine to command.

The sunlight lay golden over the city and warm breezes spread through the streets as proof that spring had finally arrived. The busy hum of traffic mixed with the sounds of my stroller. I felt my mother's presence behind me and the world welcomed me with its sounds and sights. Since I was just at the threshold of language, my mother named some of the objects we were passing, such as *"Baum," "Bus," "Hund,"* and whatever else she thought necessary to enlarge my comprehension of the world around me.

The street was wide. To my left, grass and shrubbery grew in abundance. Further ahead loomed a forbidding looking arch. The sharp contrast to the bright sunlight shimmering over trees and rooftops made this dark gray structure appear all the more sinister and threatening.

The stroller was moving closer to that gaping arch and I knew there would be no way to avoid being swallowed by this giant mouth. The muscles in my body tightened involuntarily as we went through the entrance and, once inside, I felt as though my breath was caught somewhere in my chest and would never be released. The darkness inside, the black stone walls on both sides of me, covered with soot and dampness, seemed to crush my small bones. Still not able to breathe freely, the earth seemed to stand still, and I was sure we would never get out of this monster's belly. A scream filled the pit of my stomach, but would not come out of my mouth. The rock in my throat blocked all sound. Terror unnameable, to which my mother seemed oblivious, choked my very being. I closed my eyes to shut out the horrible blackness and immediately let out a scream that bounced off the walls and came back to me like a response from the monster itself.

My fright now knew no bounds.

My mother bent down to me and her voice expressed puzzled concern, "*Was ist los, Püppchen? Was ist los?*" (What's the matter?) She stopped the carriage to stroke my head but I yelled all the more from sheer frustration for not being able to name the cause of my distress and the delay in getting out of this cavernous hole.

A thundering noise overhead. What was it?

It drowned out my screams and sent shock waves of deep rumbling sounds through the air, amplified by the narrow enclosure. I was near choking again. My mother finally understood the cause of my fear and pushed the stroller more rapidly, saying all the while, "*Schon gut, Püppchen, schon gut.*" (It's alright, Little Doll, it's alright).

Once we were outside and far enough from the black belly, she bent down again and, pointing to the thing behind us, gave it a name, "*Tunnel,*" but I merely showed my impatience to put a safe distance between me and that thing of horror. I kicked my legs, looked straight ahead of me and welcomed the warm sunlight resting on a familiar, friendlier scene.

The world is circumscribed for a small child. Each day holds new mysteries and new discoveries. People and objects pass by without a name, imprinting themselves on the mind like photographs of forgotten scenes.

The memory of this dank and dark passage lies buried in me like an underground spring, ready to erupt every time the space around me closes in and threatens to cut off my breath. Then the little girl in the stroller comes back to life and wants to break free as on that warm summer day.

A new set of sounds had invaded our family and its piercing squeals had my mother scurrying from one end of the apartment to the other. The sounds usually came at the wrong time, at night, when we were asleep, or when my mother was brushing my hair, or was dressing me in something my aunts had sewn or knitted for me. The little bundle in the wicker basket had a sixth sense for interrupting the cherished moments I had with my parents. I was told not to mind it too much, that the sounds were coming from my baby brother, Hans. I was not very interested in this new addition to our household, this wiggly, noisy little creature that looked like my baby doll, but did not at all act like her.

When he was quietly asleep and I wanted to play with him, my mother gently guided my hand away and told me I could watch him but that I was still too little to hold him. What was the use of having this stranger around if you could not play with him or at least hold him? Everyone fussed over him and tried to convince me what a pretty little brother I would have to play with when he grew older. That seemed a long time off and, for the present, he was definitely in my way, requiring far too much attention from the adults and leaving me to play by myself with my doll and wooden pushcart.

We were moving. After the birth of my brother in 1930, my parents left my grandparents' apartment across from the synagogue on Fasanenstrasse to live in their own place. Because of the Great Depression of 1929, my father had lost his job and my parents had moved in with my grandparents. Now, though my father was employed at the Stock Exchange, he could afford only a small and inexpensive apartment for the four of us. My memory tells me that it consisted of one room, the bedroom for all four of us, and a kitchen where we ate our meals. It was on the ground floor and the sun disdained to visit it.

The gloom inside reflected the gloom cast upon the world outside, when, three years later, I became an involuntary witness to the only argument I ever heard between my parents.

Their voices were raised above the usual pitch to which I was accustomed. Something about the tone and volume, the acerbity and intensity in their voices broke into my world of play so much that I began to listen to them without their noticing it. The words followed each other in terse, fragmented sentences; my father's voice especially took on a more and more aggressive tone as he was pacing the floor in short, hurried steps, gesticulating with his hands and moving his head from side to side while my mother was sitting on the bed folding laundry. She responded in a voice barely audible and feebly defensive. It sounded more like a moan, and occasionally her phrases ended with a deep sigh.

They seemed altogether oblivious to my presence, as though a five-year-old could not possibly follow their argument. I sensed vaguely that they were locked in a terrible and serious battle. Some words like "*kein Geld*" (no money), and "*helfen*" (help), then "*Hitler*" stood out from the rest until I listened more carefully and could follow the gist of their argument. I did so all the more freely once I was sure that I had become invisible to them.

"Your parents do not want to help," my father emphasized each word.

"They do as much as they can, Fritz."

"They do not like me, I know."

"You know very well that is not true."

"They would rather you had not married a Jew."

"Whose family was it that objected to our marriage?"

"They may even believe what Hitler tells them about Jews."

"That is a lie, and you know it," my mother snapped angrily.

At her last remark, my father's temper broke loose and, shouting something incoherent, he pushed her away from him as she stood up to answer him. She lost her balance and fell against the wardrobe next to the bed. I looked on, horrified and silent, not understanding the source of his fury or his pain. I hated him at that moment. My mother raised herself slowly and, her face pale with fright, her mouth tightly shut, she continued with her chores.

My father left the room. He returned minutes later and was wearing his overcoat, carrying mine on his arm.

"*Komm, Püppchen,*" he said in a voice changed from anger to sadness. "Let's go for a walk."

I was reluctant to go but did not dare to say openly that I did not want to go on a *Spaziergang* and leave my mother all alone with her pain. I looked at her, hoping that she would read my thoughts and ask my father to leave me with her. But her attention was given solely to the chore before her.

Walking in the direction of a nearby park, my father held my hand and remained silent. The park presented its usual face, with mothers pushing baby carriages, children playing or feeding the ducks in a small pond, and old folks sitting on benches, alone or chatting with companions. Everything seemed normal except that the silence between my father and me felt increasingly oppressive; I was beginning to wonder why he had brought me along at all. Then, as we were strolling along, he relaxed and started talking to himself at first so that I could not make out the words. When he remembered that I was walking beside him, he looked down at me and started talking out loud, continuing his train of thought.

"You see, *Püppchen,* I did not marry a *Putzfrau* (cleaning lady) - I married a woman. Mama hardly ever takes time to talk to me, she is always so busy cleaning - always with a broom in one hand and a dust cloth in the other. A man wants more than that."

I sensed the frustration in his voice, but I could not understand the nature of his complaint; only the words carved themselves into my mind. What had all this to do with their argument; what is wrong with my mother keeping our constricted living quarters neat and tidy? Why would he not stop talking about her in this way and expect me to take sides? I felt like a traitor to my mother and wanted to rush home to her.

My discomfort dissipated as soon as we reached home and I saw my parents talk in a more amicable way, first in whispers and then in their usual tone, as if nothing had happened.

It was not until I arrived at the age of reason that I was able to make the connection between cause and effect. My father was among the first of many Jews to lose his job in 1933 after Hitler came to power. It was the beginning of the vilification and degradation of Jews that shattered the lives of individuals and of families. The ripple effect of this touched my parents' relationship and presented a cruel test to my mother's loyalty to her Jewish husband and children. Born of non-Jewish parents, she proved again and again, like Ruth of the Bible who also had embraced the God of Israel, her unwavering devotion to husband and children of a despised people.

Huge red flags twice the height of a man, with the black swastika in a white circle, met my eyes from house fronts, lamp posts and towers all over Berlin, in stark, macabre contrast to the newly fallen snow that covered the city like a bridal veil. It was a strangely wonderful, frightening sight, this black and white and red, and the six-year-old in me felt oddly thrilled by the vibrancy of colors reminiscent of "Snow White and the Seven Dwarves." Yet I was beginning to understand that I was in no fairyland, that those who saluted these flags with their hands held high, shouting, "*Sieg Heil*," were, in my father's version, not our friends.

"When you see men in brown uniforms, do not look at them, do not make any noise to attract their attention. Be on your best behavior by being quiet," counseled my father.

When I asked him why, his response sounded gentle, "They do not like Jews."

His words cut into my memory and echoed through the years. From that day on, I avoided the men in uniforms and walked the streets as though I were mute and invisible.

Our street was half a block away from Bismarkstrasse, a favorite avenue for parades because its length ran like a lifeline through the city, while its imposing width could accommodate hundreds of spectators.

One day my father announced that there was going to be a parade of Hitler, the new Fuhrer and his staff. They were expected to ride in open limousines, in full regalia and in view of the people who would thus have a chance to see their new leader in the flesh, and shout their welcome in thunderous unison. My father explained to us that he wanted to see what all the fuss was about and to have a good look at these scoundrels. He took me with him and we stood in the fifth or sixth row of the waiting crowd. Rhythmic shouts of "*Heil! Sieg Heil!*" all along Bismarkstrasse saturated the air and beat on my eardrums. My father, taller than average, put me on his shoulders so I could look above peoples' heads at the approaching limousine. People were raising their right arms and, when the limousine was only a few yards away, there was a deafening shout again of "*Sieg, Heil,*" coming from a thousand throats, sounding as though this greeting came from one giant mouth. Next to the driver stood a man in uniform, his right arm raised full length while his head turned from side to side to acknowledge all the people who tirelessly declared their love of the Fuhrer, waving small flags and smiling happily, their eyes brimming with tears. Hitler smiled in return, a fixed smile that seemed carved on an otherwise immobile face. Those seated behind him, my father explained, were Goebbels, the thin one, and Goering, the stout one. The same smile was affixed to their faces, faces and names I would come to know better over the next twelve years.

———

As winter approached, our one-room apartment turned cold and damp. The small wood-burning stove, standing in the far left corner from the entrance, was hardly equipped to ward off the penetrating temperatures of a Berlin winter.

My mother, always of delicate health, developed a persistent cough, then pneumonia, and was finally stricken with tuberculosis.

One day she was gone.

"Mama is in the hospital," my father explained her absence, coupled with the reassurance that doctors and nurses in white uniforms were going to take care of her. The mention of white uniforms was no doubt intended to point out the contrast with the men in brown uniforms roaming the streets in search of enemies of the state.

We were making the necessary adjustments to my mother's absence when my father told us that we were going to move to another apartment two houses away, on Fritschstrasse 26. "I'm not going to bring Mama back to this rat hole." He sounded angry.

This was how we learned that our mother was coming home. The new apartment was an improvement. It was on the second floor in the *Hinterhaus* of an apartment complex and, though it did not get much sun during the day, it was provided with central heating for the winter months. Since the doctor advised my mother to sleep with the window open, she slept by herself in one of the two rooms we had. She had to follow this arrangement for the rest of her life.

My mother's return home soon put us back in our daily routine. She resumed her usual tasks as much as possible, and my father began to help out more with the household chores, a practice he continued for years to come. The scar on the left side of my mother's neck where a doctor had performed a tracheotomy was the only reminder of her ordeal and the void she had left in our lives for a brief period of time.

With all of the five pennies of my allowance, I had bought one of my favorite snacks - a bag of various cake crumbs that the bakery across the street sold to children and other cake lovers. I was sorting through them to find my favorite poppy seed cake, and had almost finished the second piece when I passed some boys I had never seen before loitering in the entrance of a house not far from our own. The words, "*Judensau*" (Jew swine), "go back where you came from," struck my ears like a foreign language. And where was I supposed to have come from who lived on the same street with these boys? It took some time before I realized that their invectives were aimed at me. The cold stare and jeering expression on one of them, looking at me directly, left me in no doubt. Mischievous boys, like the story of *Max und Moritz*, who play their pranks with gun powder and booby traps, were known to me only from picture books, but these boys were real and more than mischievous. The hate in their voices quickened my steps with sudden fear.

I ran to the safety of our home, clutching the bag with its sweet contents.

Our first grade teacher, Fräulein Opitz, came into the classroom one morning, sat down at her desk and, with her hands folded in front of her so tightly that the whites of her knuckles showed, told us with obvious embarrassment that she had to ask us a question.

"Who among you is Jewish?" The words came out low and hesitant, taking us all by surprise. I was looking around the room to see if there were any raised hands. There were none. I raised mine, not sure whether I should. Fräulein Opitz nodded her head in acknowledgment and began her lesson for the day.

My father was home when I returned from school and my first question to him was, "Papa, am I Jewish?"

"*Ja, natürlich*, but why do you ask?" There was a faint smile on his face. When I told him what had happened, his smile changed to a frown.

A few days later, Fräulein Opitz had another task: to recruit girls for the BDM (Organization for German Girls). "Who would like to join?" she asked the class after she had described the various activities the organization had to offer: outings to the woods, sports events and singing popular folk tunes. I raised my hand with several other girls. She asked to see me alone after class. Left alone in the classroom, she told me that the organization was closed to Jews. The tone of affection and regret in her voice did little to alleviate my feeling of being an outcast.

What makes a Jew different from others? At that age, I could not understand the reason for my exclusion.

As I remember it, my father rose early each morning, left the apartment as though to go to work, but would arrive home tired and discouraged to tell my mother, "All doors are closed to me." The figure of my father, his shoulders slumped, his lips drawn tight to hold in his tears and anger, became a familiar image throughout the war. My mother, managing a faint smile, would reply to his despondency with warm reassurance "Tomorrow will be better."

Ever afterward, as the tomorrows grew darker, she never faltered in her encouragement and optimism for better days to come.

Despite the financial hardships his unemployment created, my mother always managed to put food on the table so that we lacked for nothing. Her expertise as a cook had its crowning moments in those days when the budget spelled calamity. Her potato pancakes, stuffed yeast or potato dumplings, her lentil soup and noodle casserole, never lost their taste and appeal for us. On days when her meager allowance would allow it, she treated us to her famous Hungarian goulash or *Kasslerbraten*. She seemed to have myriad ways of preparing potatoes, and we were never without puddings or cakes for holidays. Her meals took away the gloom and replaced it with warmth and hope.

My father, meanwhile, took his unemployment as a personal defeat rather than what it really was: Hitler's war against Jews, as announced in 1933 with the boycott of Jewish businesses. My father spoke constantly of being a beggar, dependent on *Almosen*, alms given him by welfare agencies. His humiliation at being divested of his patriarchal responsibilities was complete. A husband and father has to provide for his family, and he was prevented from doing it through work.

When his spirits were lowest, he bolstered them by showing us pictures of better days, of him sitting in the back of his Pierce Arrow with the chauffeur in the front seat, or a picture of himself and my mother standing beside his small french sports car. "*Ja*, your Papa was once a successful man, you see," he would sigh, shaking his head dejectedly.

He then put the pictures away with other piles of yesterday's memories.

The view I formed of my father during those difficult times took on a dual nature: the shadowy picture of a man at the height of his success, courting the woman of his choice, our mother, a girl from a working class family, in high style, full of promise and joy, and then the man crushed by circumstances not of his own making, burdened with a sense of failure and impotence. Yet he clung to his ideal of a paterfamilias and remained a source of safety for us, a transmitter of knowledge and tradition, and our moral guide for things human and divine. With his tall figure and firm walk, his refreshing sense of humor that he retained to the end, he was still able to build a wall of protection for his children against a world that grew more hostile day by day. But there appeared cracks in that wall, threatening to weaken its structure and needing constant repair from the people around him, especially from my mother. She never tired of sustaining his flagging spirit with her calm fortitude and selfless devotion. She went about her daily business with unfailing diligence; I never heard her utter a word of complaint or discouragement. Only her eyes, deep set and golden brown, would at times show the sadness she felt for the cruel destiny that now united her with a doomed people. There was an ironic twist to the reversal in their roles. My father's loss seemed to be my mother's gain. From my father's financial ruin sprang my mother's spiritual strength. Perhaps her working class background made the transition to straitened circumstances easier for her than for my father, coming from an affluent past and its easy comforts. They seemed, at any rate, to complement each other well to meet the exacting demands placed on Jewish life in Hitler's Berlin.

―――――

Berlin was putting on its Sunday best. Feverish activities in preparation for the 1936 Olympic Games were present everywhere with the now familiar fanfare of speeches and parades. Flags from many nations waved in the wind to impress the natives and the international community. The bullies in the Nazi party adopted a modicum of civilized behavior and even Hitler had become a "wolf in sheep's clothing" and suspended temporarily his *Hassreden*, his mad ranting against Jews. Signs of "Jews not wanted," were taken off. We breathed somewhat easier, but my father kept reminding us that Germany's honeymoon with other nations would eventually be over, and that divorce proceedings would inevitably follow.

I was eight years old and felt relatively free from harm and hatred. I experienced no harassment from my peers or teachers. My classmates included me in their games and my teachers treated me no differently from their non-Jewish students. For all appearances, I blended in and no one knew that I was taking Hebrew lessons in our spacious and beautiful synagogue on Fasanenstrasse, where I practiced my reading skills during services, and where we could still worship the God of Israel.

Whatever sinister signs erupted in the body politic, my family members held my world together with their loving concern and attention, although one discordant note was beginning to disturb the quiet tenor of my life. My cousin Klaus, two years my senior, was the "Aryan" son of my mother's sister. He was an avid sports fan and spoke incessantly about the Olympics, not merely as an international competition, but as a national celebration of the superior quality of German athletes participating in the games. The companion of my earliest childhood years, trusted and admired, was moving further and further away from me and closer to the ranks of ardent nationalists.

The Berlin Olympics touched our family only peripherally. They were soon overshadowed by another event of more immediate importance. My paternal grandmother was gravely ill. We were given to understand that she might not live much longer. She was in the hospital and, my father told us one day, she wanted to see her grandchildren. Sensing some dark urgency in her request, my first response was to say, "No, I don't want to see her," afraid to look at the woman I had known all my life as "Oma" in her deteriorating state. My father intuited my reluctance and assured me that "Oma still looks like Oma."

The day we went to see her at the hospital, I stopped at the door to her room to see my grandmother lying in bed, propped up on pillows with medical instruments nearby. Pitiable moans were coming from her and, though the woman did indeed look like Oma, as my father had promised, she was paler, thinner, and her immobility made her seem no longer a part of the living. Her breath came in short gasps so that I involuntarily withdrew a few steps into the hallway. My father noticed and motioned me to come closer, trying hard to encourage me with a smile, but barely managing a sad grimace. I saw him bending down to her and straining to hear what she wanted to tell him. Then she gave me a faint smile, it came and went like the flicker of a match. I kept looking at this woman who was suddenly a stranger to me, or had she always been a stranger? Who was she, so helpless now, so alone, so distant? My father whispered something to her, then made ready to leave. I wanted to say "*Auf Wiedersehen*," wondering whether those were the right words to say.

We left the hospital, and the pale woman in the white bed was soon just a fading memory.

A few days had passed when my father entered the bedroom, dressed in his pants and undershirt, his hair uncombed, his shoulders stooped. He sat down on the lower bunk bed and before he spoke, I knew already what he had to tell us.

"I have some sad news..." he began, unable to go on. He spoke haltingly and with an obvious effort to keep back the tears, "Oma died last night. I went to see her but she was no longer able to recognize me. She died peacefully... she left us... forever." At the last words he covered his face with his hands and broke into sobs, stopping only to mutter, "My dear mother... *meine geliebte Mutter*."

What could I say to this big, broken man, my father, whose grief welled up from a place deep within, setting me apart? I could only watch, frightened and stunned by the vastness of his sorrow in which he seemed to wander all alone. I could not follow him in his pain. I only sensed that the loss of his mother was the loss of a world to him, irretrievable and final. As he sat there, all hunched over, crying inconsolably, he was her little boy again, lost and terrified at being left alone, just like the time I was lost from my mother in the huge department store.

I felt like a trespasser into some forbidden territory in my father's heart, and his weeping was unsettling to me. To hide my discomfort, I pulled the bed covers closer to me and wanted my own mother. I grieved more for my father's loss than for the loss of a grandmother who, now that she was gone, seemed to have touched my life but lightly, like a warm summer breeze which delights for a moment, but whose passing we do not mourn.

My father's loss of his mother rendered him an orphan, since his father had died in 1929 when I was barely two years old. I have no memory associated with my paternal grandfather, only two photographs.

I was making friends with a girl named Ilse who lived in our apartment building. She was not Jewish and we were both attending the third grade. Our windows faced each other across the backyard of our apartment complex. On evenings when we could no longer play out on the street, we "talked" with our flashlights to assure each other of our continued presence.

On good days, after we had done our homework, we joined other children from the neighborhood and played many of the games common to childhood. My favorite games were ball games, either those involving one or two people which required just enough space on the front wall of our house for bouncing the ball in fancy configurations, or games that involved opposite teams, like *Völkerball* (volleyball), which we played in the middle of the street. Traffic then was almost non-existent.

Ilse was indifferent to my being Jewish and felt a certain affinity with me, the outcast. Freely, though in whispers, she referred to the brown shirts as *diese Kerle*, those scoundrels, an expression, no doubt, she must have heard from her father, who had instilled in her a distinct dislike of the Nazis. He worked for the *Reichsbahn*, the state railroad and, in order to keep his job, had to give up his former affiliation with the Communist Party. Ilse confided in me that he nevertheless had not given up his old ideals. Every time there were rumors of another raid on former Socialists or Communists by the Nazis, another person taken prisoner or tortured, Ilse voiced her anger. I, who had been drilled in keeping silent, had to ask her more than once to keep her thoughts and feelings hidden from the public. I told her what I had learned from my parents as a five-year-old, and which had made a vivid impression upon me, *Die Wände haben Ohren*, the walls have ears. When I told her about Fräulein Opitz's reply to my interest in joining the BDM, she just shrugged her shoulders and said something like, "Why would anyone want to join this army of crooks? My parents have forbidden me to join it."

Ilse and I found secret places where we could talk more freely, though always cautiously. We shared our grievances about teachers, classmates, parents, other relatives and, in my case, my cousin Klaus from whom I became more and more estranged. Ilse listened sympathetically and, as if to compensate for Klaus's growing fervor for National Socialism, she took a lively interest in Judaism, especially historical events connected with Jewish holidays. The story of Chanukah intrigued her particularly, and she wanted to own a menorah. When I told her that it would be against the law, even for Jews, to own one, she started on one of her diatribes against the regime and repeated what so many people I knew were still saying, "Hitler can't last long. *Er ist doch verrückt*, he is crazy." I wanted to believe her but knew from conversations at home that many Jews were leaving Germany because they had lost hope for Jewish life in Germany.

I listened to my parents speak about emigration, but it was an abstract issue for me. My immediate world of family and friends still seemed safe and comfortable. I felt insulated from the voices screaming hatred.

––––––

It is a warm and sunny day. Ilse and I are playing in front of our house. Two boys our age approach us with swaggering steps and a mischievous glint in their eyes. My body tenses as I watch them with mounting suspicion, knowing that they are scheming something because I had heard them tease Hans for being Jewish. One of them is whispering something to the other.

"Hey, you, Jew swine," the same one says, looking at me. "Can you say something in Jewish?"

"It's not called Jewish," I correct him, "It's called Hebrew."

"Don't get smart with us, you dirty Jew," the same boy replies. "Then say something in Hebrew, the dirty Jew language."

"All I know is prayers," I answer him, "and I'm not supposed to say them unless..."

My objection is met with a raised fist, and incites them to further taunts and threats. When I try to reason with them, they laugh all the more and threaten to beat me up if I do not comply with their demands. By now they have pushed me into a corner of the entrance to our house and reiterate their demands more pugnaciously, leaving me no way out. Ilse is watching helplessly, afraid of retaliation if she interferes. To her timid, "Leave her alone," they hiss, "Halt's Maul! Shut your trap!"

There remains nothing for me to do but to say the Credo for Jews, our *Sh'ma*. When they are not satisfied with that, I recite the blessing I hear my father say over the bread.

"Sounds like the pigs you are... oink, oink," is the response of the more aggressive one, and both break into laughter as they turn around to leave.

Any incentive to continue our game is gone. I go upstairs. Alone in the bedroom that I share with my father and brother, I ask God's forgiveness for my sacrilege, my cowardice for using God's name in vain.

The gloom the political situation cast over our lives was not able to dispel some of its brighter moments. One of these was the traditional laundry day, *Grosse Wäsche*, once a month. On the morning of *Grosse Wäsche*, my mother came into our bedroom before we were up and said cheerily, "Time to get up - I need to strip your beds." *Grosse Wäsche* was an unfailing ritual among housewives. Each apartment house was therefore provided with facilities under the roof. Watching my mother go through the various stages of this rite, I thought of her as a priestess purifying her temple, for the home was my mother's sanctuary.

I followed her up the stairs into the attic, where I waited for her directions. "The sheets go into the soaking trough," she pointed to a wooden, rectangular tub where some linens were already soaking in a sluggish gray liquid. I put items I had helped carry upstairs into the trough. Next to it stood another tub of the same size full of rinsing water into which the linens went after a night's soaking. Across from these was the *pièce de résistance* of the washroom, a thing of awe to me - a large round heavy copper metal container that rested on a bed of red hot coals. The soaked and rinsed linens eventually went in there, left to boil until they were free of the month-old dirt and germs. Every item that went into this cauldron was made of sturdy enough cotton or linen to withstand the harsh treatment of heat and cleansing agents. Placed close to it was another large wooden tub with rinse water; it was no small feat to take out each piece from the boiling water and deposit it in the rinsing water. My mother used a long wooden instrument, shaped like an oar, and deftly lifted each piece from the boiling water to transfer it to the tub of fresh water, her face covered with tiny beads of perspiration. There were hoses throughout the washroom leading from faucets to the different tubs so as to ensure a constant exchange of dirty with fresh water. The floor was smooth and of a whitish grey color from years of soapy water being spilled onto it then sent down large drains. Wooden platforms about five inches high were scattered on the floor and prevented the water from soaking your feet.

While waiting for the water to reach its desired temperature, we would go downstairs to the apartment where my mother would busy herself with smaller items to be washed either by hand or boiled in a large pot on top of the stove. While that was under way, we went back to the attic to prepare the finished items to be hung on the clotheslines underneath the roof.

The air through the open windows dried them and permeated everything with its freshness.

The washroom had meanwhile filled with steam, smelling of soap and the various textiles. Pulling out the soaked linens was the part I liked best because my mother usually asked my help in wringing out the water. I held one end of a sheet while she twisted the other. Then followed the high point of the operation, dropping the pieces into the boiling cauldron. I had to climb onto a stool in order to watch the linens twirl and turn in the bubbling water. It was as though I were looking at a pot of goulash cooking on our kitchen stove. My mother stirred the linen with her oar as a wet strand of her hair fell out of her kerchief and clung to her cheek, flushed and moist from the heat. Then she turned to me and smiling, told me that she did not need me anymore until it was time to press the clean laundry in the rolling press in my grandmother's *Seifenladen*, a soap store.

The rolling press was a huge cylindrical drum filled with heavy rocks that emitted a rumbling sound like distant thunder when the machine was in motion. I would watch my mother with fascination as she placed a wrinkled piece of linen into one side and pull it out, straight and smooth, on the other. I had trouble imagining how this monster of rock and steel had been transplanted into my grandparents' bedroom where it stood in jarring juxtaposition to the two beds on the opposite wall, with their soft eiderdown coverlets bulging like fleecy clouds.

A permanent odor of damp linens was at all times present in this room, subsuming any personal smell which a bedroom might have. It always struck me as odd how my grandparents could so easily plant such a monstrous and musty smelling piece of equipment in the most intimate place for a married couple.

What dreams could such a room inspire?

The *Seifenladen* store belonged to my grandmother, but the management of it had been in the hands of my mother's sister, Tante Liesel, for as long as I could remember. She was also in charge of the care of my grandmother who needed constant assistance from the people around her. She was confined to her wheelchair in the kitchen due to ulcerous varicose veins, a condition she had contracted after years of standing on a cold cement floor behind the counter to serve her customers. Cause and effect were discovered too late to bring about a reversal of this debilitating condition. Even though I was aware of the history of her disability, my childish imagination dwelled only in the present and the mysterious world of grown-up activity.

My grandmother's *Seifengeschäft* held for me all the allure of an adult world not yet within my grasp. I saw none of the hardships, the unremitting labor of long hours and few rewards, but only the magic of shiny, brass-plated measuring weights for the old-fashioned scale, the exchange of money from one hand to another as I watched my aunt wait on her customers with a smile for each customer and friendly inquiries about personal or local news. The world of weights and numbers seemed remote and wondrous to me. My aunt, who was in charge of it all, compared in my mind to a reigning queen.

It was only after business hours or on holidays that this world became mine for a brief space of time, when I was allowed to experiment with the various-sized brass weights shining like gold, trying to bring one side of the scales into equilibrium with the other. Then also was I free to touch and investigate the different articles in the store and pretend that I was the proud owner of all these riches. Those were halcyon days which gave me my first sense of adult activity and power.

My mother was part of this world on days when she took over the care of the store and her invalid mother in order to give her sister a few hours of respite from her daily drudgery. After my aunt had stepped out of her Cinderella clothes and transformed herself into a *grand dame*, she left for her night out. I was allowed to stay behind the counter with my mother and to be known as the daughter of Frieda Kuhn, a small satellite in the orbit of her life away from our home.

In these environs, though crammed and devoid of any sunlight, my childhood was free to flourish like poppies in an open field.

———

The constant attempts I made as a child trying to balance the two ends of that scale developed into more than a childhood game, for it is perhaps from those days that at times I think of our fortunes as determined by a metaphysical scale, tipping down one lot for us one time, then raising it another time until perfect parity is established. Thus, our good days and our bad days, our good deeds and our bad deeds, will be weighed against each other by a mysterious calculator whose ultimate logic escapes us, except to help us realize that the sum of our earthly fortunes may eventually balance.

In 1936, the same year my father lost his mother, he asked us to sit around the dinner table for a family talk.

"I have decided," he began, "to take you out of your school... to transfer you..."

"No," I broke in impetuously, "I don't want to leave my school and my friends there. I like it."

"I know, Rita," my father said softly. "The principal and I discussed it and we decided it would be better for you to attend a Jewish school where you can be among your own."

He continued with his explanation and broke my resistance entirely when he mentioned the name of the school he had chosen for us. It was housed in the synagogue in Fasanenstrasse where we frequented services and where my parents had been married. The prospect of going there and making the school my intellectual home, as it had already become the cradle of my spiritual beginnings, quickly erased any regrets I felt for losing old friends. I would make new ones from among those cast out from their German schools.

The only adjustment I would have to make was the long walk from home to school, fourteen blocks unless I took the streetcar. Ten of these blocks were along Kantstrasse, one of the main streets of Berlin that was lined with a variety of stores, many of them Jewish. The only time I minded walking all this distance was in winter, when temperatures dropped below zero and froze your nostrils together. Hands and feet would be stiff with the cold and the classroom offered little relief, since Jewish schools suffered more than others from a deplorable shortage of fuel.

My father had been right when he told us that we would "feel better among your own." Aside from subjects required by the state, like German history, I could now learn Hebrew, Jewish history, Hebrew folk songs, and dances. I was also able to express my feelings, however cautiously, to friends about the growing danger for us.

The school, the classroom, the teachers, the students, all constituted a small world nestled into the larger one, where no flags with swastikas, no Nazi salutes and songs disturbed the quiet unfolding of our minds. Our games were free from intrusions by hostile peers. Here we were judged and, whenever necessary, chastised by our own people; the only fear that ruled was that of incurring the wrath of one of the stricter teachers. One teacher in particular, a Dr. Schwarz, would preface his punishments with a warning, *Wie es in Wald hineinschallt, so schallt es heraus* (The sound entering the forest, leaves it the same way, or, What goes around, comes around).

During that time, I also learned there were two parts of me. I was one person to family and friends, I was another to strangers on the street. There was constant tension between pride and humiliation, between a sense of my own identity fostered in the home and at school, and the verbal assaults coming from an antagonistic world which openly proclaimed its hatred of Jews from posters, speeches, and the media.

Jewish life in Berlin was in peril. That knowledge was like the slow advance of a deadly disease.

The voices of the past, of King David and King Solomon, Esther and Ruth still sounded strong in our ears, but they were in danger of being drowned out by the thunderous speeches of Hitler and Goebbels railing against the Jewish menace. The more we recited our Hebrew in school, the louder those other voices grew and carried others with them. There was no hiding from these voices of hate and paranoia except by redirecting our energies to the daily routine of living.

No one could foresee the time when the protective walls of the synagogue would crumble and leave us exposed to the fury beyond them.

Hans and I were fighting again and, predictably, as the older sister, I had to take the blame for it. I chafed at this injustice and refused to see my part in the feud. As the firstborn, I saw nothing wrong with asserting my 'superiority' over my sibling brother and of devising ways to be in control. As soon as we passed the normal boundaries of mere bickering, when our tempers and voices reached a full crescendo, my mother would have to stop what she was doing and mediate between us, although she hardly ever witnessed what motivated us to start a screaming contest.

"Must you always annoy him?" My mother turned to me with an angry face.

"He started it," I defended myself, knowing that it would be utterly useless to try and convince her.

It was a revelation when I realized that being older had definite disadvantages, since the difference of just two years ascribed to me a mental cunning against which the seeming innocence of my younger brother was thought to be powerless. In time, I got used to an image of myself as the troublemaker, the mean older sister, while Hans was cast as the *Goldkind*, the pretty little boy with the golden curls flattering his baby face out of which his big blue eyes looked at the world in wonder and guilelessness. Hans's pictures appeared in magazines for parents or sold as postcards, always with a pensive expression on his face and questioning eyes. He wore his golden curls long into his fourth year, both for show and because they covered his slightly protruding ears. When they had to be cut to fit a boy's image, Hans had to sleep with his ears taped to the side of his head in the vain hope that one day they would lie flattened to his head.

Even angels can't be perfect.

———

Hans and I were irreconcilable rivals for the approval, attention, and affection of the adults in our family. How to get their attention without forfeiting their approval was a game I had not yet mastered, especially when I emerged from our battles as the villain and was asked each time to apologize for introducing so much friction into our home. Apologize for what, I bristled. Apologies were thought to set matters right, whereas for me, they only added to the imbalance of right and wrong. An apology seemed to me an empty gesture to solving a deeper problem, though I was hard put to give a name to it. I could not apologize and thought it more humiliating than being punished. I preferred my parents' anger to a false peace.

Yet, despite our continual squabbles, our parents trusted us enough to leave us in the care of the lady next door on evenings when they went out. On those nights we talked ourselves to sleep, happy not to have our father come into our room to check whether we were asleep every five minutes. After we had said our prayers, my father turned off the lights for the night, a wordless message that there was to be no more talking. Though the day's activities may have ceased, my body and mind had difficulty obeying the parental command of "Go to sleep." I wondered every time how he could tell that we were not asleep, until I figured out that he knew it by the fluttering of our eyelids. The censure his checking produced had, of course, the opposite effect: I lay wide awake in nervous anticipation of his next visit and the rising threat in his voice. It was never followed by punishment, but the tone of his voice, grave and urgent, was like the Prophets of the Bible, or what I thought they must have sounded like to the offending children of Israel.

After my parents had gone out and the lady across from us had told us that she would be checking on us occasionally, Hans and I began to talk, first in whispers and, when we tired of that, in a more normal tone of voice, knowing from past experience that our neighbor would leave us alone for the rest of the night. Hans and I had, nevertheless, an internalized censor so that we never dared to get out of bed for fear of some invisible monitor between us and parental authority.

Despite our acrimony, there existed a bond between Hans and me that transcended our petty spats. We told each other stories, griped about teachers, troublesome classmates, and exchanged grievances about the figures of authority in our life. Having exhausted these topics, we turned to speculations about the existence of the spirit world, how it may impinge on our own human world. Once this question was out in the open, it seemed as though some small demon had entered me and goaded me to play some cruel trick on Hans.

"Did you hear that?" I would ask in as close to a terrified voice as I could manage, half believing in the imaginary sound myself.

"No... what is it?" he asked with genuine fear.

"There... there it is again, over in that corner, behind the wardrobe," I insisted relentlessly, spurred on by his obvious fright.

"I can't hear it. What does it sound like?" he asked, convinced of its existence and sounding more alarmed.

Not really knowing how to answer him, I just crawled under the covers with a horrified "Ooooh," which he imitated by pulling the pillow over his head and asked in a muffled tone, "Can you still hear it?"

No matter how often we played this game, and I had to make up different versions each time, Hans fell right into it and acted out his fear so genuinely that I often ended up being just as scared as he was of these figments of my imagination, which had suddenly turned into actual presences. The spell was on me as well and I wondered whether a simple word of mine could dispel it.

"Wait a minute," I said after a while, "I think they are gone," as if it were a magic formula to drive them away from our room. When I thought I had banished these unwelcome visitors from our bedroom, I became the good sister in turn, protective and concerned by reassuring my brother that the spirits would never hurt good children because God would keep all evil away from us. Believing this myself, we would both fall asleep.

Good news! Finally! My father had found work after four bitter years. His new job was going to be in the emigration department of the Jewish Council in Oranienburger Strasse. We stormed him with questions of who qualified, what it takes to emigrate, and whether he could now help his own family. His response was the same each time we asked; first a smile at our ready confidence in his newly acquired authority to facilitate emigration for Jews, followed by a shrug of his shoulders, a quizzical look on his face.

"Where do you think we could find the money and the sponsor? We need both, you know, and those who are leaving Germany are those who have the means for it."

Ever since my grandmother's death in 1936, we had talked about the possibility of emigration, for my father would never have considered it as long as his mother was alive and ailing. The obstacles of obtaining money and a sponsor remained as sad reminders of our impoverished circumstances. Only the hope that the conditions for exit permits might become more lenient encouraged our talks about a brighter future elsewhere.

My mother put aside money as before, hiding it in the top drawer of the large sideboard in the dining room. It was her open secret, her treasure nestled away from view with no need to lock it, for no other safeguard was needed than our knowledge that there began our lifeline. Whenever I saw my mother near the drawer, removing or adding money to this source of our household finances, I saw her endowed with some special power to be the guardian of the threshold between sufficiency and destitution. I secretly wished that her little pot of gold would never be empty, but replenish itself miraculously as in fairy tales.

Who knows, I thought, perhaps one day there might be enough in that box to take us to America.

The land of our dreams, America, where the hope for freedom for Jews was a living reality, was receding further and further into the distance for us by more than the thousands of miles of ocean and land. We knew that many other shores were inaccessible to us as well. We then turned our attention and expectations to what was nearest at hand and drew comfort from family and friends. The news my mother brought home one day offered us one such haven from the ever-lengthening shadows gathering around us.

"Guess what!" she said excitedly upon entering our apartment, smiling at each of us as she took off her coat and put away her pocketbook. Now that my father had found employment, smiles came easier for everyone. My mother had just come from a visit to her cousins, whom we called Tante Emmi and Tante Martha, who told her that they had bought a plot of land in Biesdorf on which they planned eventually to build a house.

"Biesdorf?" I asked, at first more disappointed than glad. "Where is that?"

"It's about thirty minutes on the S-Bahn from here," my mother was quick to calm me when she heard the anxious tone in my voice. "They will be there a fortnight from now and want us to come visit them on Sunday."

Our excitement now was genuine and unreserved. We wanted to know every possible detail my mother knew about the place. All she could tell us was that it was in a quiet place in the country, that the plot was large enough for building a roomy house, and that there was a big garden for growing fruit and vegetables.

"You'll be able to judge for yourselves when we go visit them," my mother smiled again, this time with a certain aura of mystery, which added to our impatience for Sunday.

On the appointed Sunday, we took the S-Bahn to our destination, called Berlin-Biesdorf. All through the ride, I had noticed a gradual change in the scenery from one station to the next. From the familiar sight of four-story apartment buildings, stacked close together with hardly a tree visible, from factories belching smoke from their tall chimneys and a landscape where the colors of grey, brown, or a dirty white predominated, we came to an area where the buildings had dwindled to one-family homes surrounded by gardens where industry had been ousted and the land dressed itself in colors of green, red, and yellow. Sunlight spread itself generously over houses and fields, skipping playfully from rooftop to rooftop, crowning trees and grass with golden rays that met few obstacles.

"A few more stops, and we'll be there," my mother announced, breaking into my reverie.

The landscape changed again and the colors were less vibrant but more verdant in their earthiness. The spaces between habitations were larger and appeared in clusters, spotted with orchards and fields in between. Some of the houses had shrunk to mere cottages while the gardens and fields had grown larger.

When we finally got off at our station, we had to walk along country roads before we arrived at my aunts' new property on Eckermannstrasse 140. As we passed through the countryside, dotted with small cottages that looked like oversized doll houses, I felt already as though I had entered another world, another country, for as far as the eye could see there was only the sky and the land beneath it lying in silent expectation. Even the air was different, as though it had gone through the laundry, leaving it smelling fresh and clean with a faint odor of damp earth.

There were no flags anywhere, no soldiers marching, no black boots patrolling the streets, and no ugly slogans from sign posts or advertising pillars.

Such quiet was here that it seemed the whole world was celebrating the Sabbath. Occasionally we saw people at work in their gardens or heard the sound of a rooster or a dog barking. The sky stretched on into unknown territory and the wind carried a soft message of peace and friendship. Hatred seemed to have been banished from this sleepy spot on the earth.

We turned into Eckermannstrasse and passed a few houses when my mother cried out, "Here we are!" We stopped in front of a fenced-in plot with fruit trees lining the opposite sides of a garden where flowers and vegetation of various kinds grew in wild profusion. A bell announced our arrival and then we saw one of my aunts walking along a small garden path to open the gate.

"*Na, willkommen*," Tante Emmi said smiling, and guided us through the lush growth at a leisurely pace, pointing out the variety of flowers and fruit trees, and where they planned to grow vegetables and berries. The twenty trees along the sides of the garden were cherry trees, she explained, and promised a good harvest.

We had meanwhile come to the far end of the garden and saw an object altogether at odds with its surroundings. It was an old railroad car, long and dark gray from age, with small windows already covered with curtains, which created a cheerful picture of domesticity in contrast to the somber gray of the exterior.

"Come in," my aunt invited us, as she climbed the three steps into the interior of the car as any conductor had done before her. My aunts both laughed in amusement at our open-mouthed bewilderment when we stepped inside and beheld what appeared to be a life-sized doll house. The space inside was divided into three sections. We entered through the kitchen, then stepped into a larger room that was both a sitting and a dining room, until we finally ended up in the bedroom, which was large enough to accommodate two beds and a wardrobe. I felt like Goldilocks in the house of the three bears. I never wanted to leave this place; it seemed so much better suited for a child than for an adult.

"There is no bathroom here," one of my aunts said matter-of-factly, injecting a bit of realism into my fantasy.

Before I could form the question, "But where do you...?" she took my hand and led me outside into another corner of the garden where there stood a small wooden structure in the shape of a small tool shed. She pointed to it with a brief, "There it is," and opened the door. There was indeed a toilet inside, if it deserved such a name, for what I saw was nothing more than a rectangular wooden box with a hole in the middle. I felt a slight shudder going down my spine as I thought of having to use this facility, practically out in the open with some creepy crawly creatures for company, possibly hiding at the bottom of the hole. I thought of the many times I'd met with an emergency on one of our long hikes in the woods when I had to squat on the ground behind some bush. That seemed infinitely preferable to this construction.

We made a tour of the rest of the garden and I found a swing hanging from the thick branch of one of the fruit trees and immediately claimed it for myself. I swung higher and higher, imagining that my feet were touching the blue sky and I was leaving the earth behind on wings I had suddenly grown. Tante Emmi, my favorite aunt, promised to keep it there for our use any time we would come for a visit.

There seemed so much to explore in this wild, wonderful garden, giving freely of its wealth to body and soul. Here, I imagined, was the closeness to nature that must have existed for our first parents who heard God walking in the garden. A re-enactment of that time seemed possible here, far from the turmoil of the city and the shouts of *"Heil Hitler."* Perhaps this spot was blessed and only goodness could flourish here.

When it was time to leave, I refused to go back to that other place, that other life where I had to avoid attracting the attention of the men in brown uniforms with their death's-heads scowling at each passerby.

The place my aunts had chosen for their new home reflected all the qualities I loved in them: their steady warmth, their unflinching generosity, their unassuming ways, and their cheerful support, especially in dark times. I felt closer to Tante Emmi who was akin to my mother in temperament and personality. Both had the same softness of manner and speech coming from an understanding and compassionate heart. Tante Martha was more like Tante Liesel: somewhat brusque and matter-of-fact in dealing with daily realities, generous with her talent as a seamstress, sewing me dresses from materials she knew I liked best, like those *mit Blümchen* (with small flowers).

Tante Emmi would lavish her talents on embroidering some of the outfits her sister had made, often to my specifications. Both of them catered to my natural vanity and helped rescue my self-esteem, crumbling from the scathing invectives of *"Judensau,"* and "dirty Jew" thrown at us. It was she who indulged me in more than my fetish for pretty dresses. She had detected my greater need for mental nourishment and encouraged my love of reading by granting me access to their copious library, which I approached like an archeologist looking for historic treasures. It proved to be a source of spiritual sustenance for me during trials yet to come.

Both aunts were telephone operators in the city. Their choice of a new home away from urban turmoil coincided with everyone's need for an escape to a world where love and laughter, food for body and soul, were norms governing this secluded spot on earth.

More and more Jewish children were leaving German schools voluntarily or by compulsion. Jewish students were barred from attending German universities anywhere within the Reich by order of the state. This was, as my father put it, "The sterilization of Jewish intellect," a grim portent that its youth was to be cut off from having a future. His voice, bitter whenever he told us of new Nazi measures taken against Jews, could no longer conceal from us the grim nature of our situation and his fear for our uncertain future under the current regime. Talks about emigration increased, but so too grew the feeling of despondency whenever we considered the unlikelihood of it ever happening to our family.

As the black boots marched on and our ears grew accustomed to the sound, our attention turned more inward to the immediate circle of family and friends.

Children who had left German schools came to our school in Fasanenstrasse and took the place of those more fortunate ones emigrating to Palestine, England, America or elsewhere to join relatives. Many left behind them grandparents, aunts, uncles, cousins, close friends, and took with them the agonizing question of whether or not they would ever see them again. Sheer force of necessity severed family ties and, in most cases, they were broken for all time when the ones left behind fell into the clutches of those enacting the Final Solution. When we said our farewell to some of our classmates, I did so with great ambivalence. I felt both relief and regret for not being one of them; relief at not having to leave the familiar for the unfamiliar, and regret for not being able to leave known dangers for safer places of which we heard from former classmates.

Children who came to us from their German schools related tales of a different kind, filled with examples of verbal abuse and, in some cases, of physical assaults from bullies of the Hitler Youth who echoed the favorite slogans of their mentors, familiar to all of us, "*Judensau*," "*Stinkjude*," and "*Juden raus*."

One of our new classmates, a boy small for his age, told us that a boy dressed in the uniform of a Hitler Youth had approached him in the school yard and, with his right arm raised, shouted at him, "*Heil Hitler!* Repeat after me, *Heil Hitler*, or I'll sock you one." When the Jewish boy refused on grounds that it was illegal for Jews to use this greeting, the Hitler Youth pushed him to the ground and would have kicked him if one of the teachers watching the scene had not intervened. Angered by that, he vented his frustration on the boy lying on the ground by hissing at him, prophetically, "Yeah, and soon it will be illegal for you shit Jews to live on German soil. *Heil Hitler!*"

Stories like this grew in frequency and their threatening nature fostered in us a greater solidarity than is usual among youngsters, so that we seldom argued among ourselves, careful to avoid open expressions of hostility. Whatever frustrations or resentments we had were released on our teachers rather than our peers. We found solace and a semblance of normalcy in our lessons, our friendships, and our childhood games. Through them we held the larger world at bay most of the time, though when it cut into our lives, it inflicted wounds as sharp as the thrust of a dagger.

Chapter 2

Broken Glass, Broken Lives

Their feet run to evil
And they make haste to shed
Innocent blood.
—Isaiah 59:7

Any casual observer from a foreign country visiting Berlin in 1938 might
have said that Berliners were doing quite well; that there were jobs for
everyone; that the city served up a cultural menu to suit the tastes of a
wide spectrum of people: from opera buffs to cabaret hoppers, from ballet
connoisseurs to fox-trot dancers; that Adolf Hitler, in short, was keeping his promises to the German people. Only the more discerning person
might have noticed that something was out of balance; that the city was
verging on schizophrenia in its treatment of an important minority of its
citizenry. Jews were rapidly being pushed aside from the main artery of
its cultural, intellectual, and economic life. Berlin, these observers would
have concluded, was a divided city, and their prognosis might have been
the opposite of the prevailing perception of its well-being: that underneath

the city's gaiety and economic boom, the paranoid hatred of Jews was the antecedent of its future destruction.

Those targeted by this hatred and some far-seeing critics of the government's totalitarian policies were able to look beyond the glittering surface of lavish parades and pompous speeches; they trembled for the future of Germany. Communists and other opponents of the regime agreed with Ernst Thaelmann; that voting for Hitler was equivalent to voting for war. For professing such sentiments they languished in prisons or concentration camps.

Jews and non-Jews opposed to Hitler were planning their future away from their homeland, not knowing when, if ever, they might return. Jews who were leaving Germany told my father that *Die Blütezeit für Juden in Deutschland ist vorüber* (the heyday for Jews in Germany has passed).

The daily behavior of Berliners had changed ever since the brown shirts and Hitler's elite guards set the guidelines for what they considered appropriate expressions of respect for them and their Führer. People no longer greeted each other in public with the customary *Guten Tag*, but instead raised their arms for the required salute of *Heil Hitler*. Many did so enthusiastically, others half-heartedly, and those who insisted on the traditional form of greeting were often subject to severe rebukes, verging on threats. It was considered as serious an opposition to the government as overt acts of resistance.

Men in uniforms, their arm bands flaunting the swastika, marched in precision goosesteps with black boots swinging high, banners swaying in the wind which carried their songs to willing and unwilling ears.

Whether Berliners liked it or not, they all had to listen to the same drummer.

Away from all this delirium, I found a happy hiding place in my school on Fasanenstrasse, where teachers and administrators provided us with a full curriculum of classes to occupy and nurture our minds and to inspire pride in our ancient heritage. We looked to some Bible figures and to Jewish history for guidance and for strength. We needed to believe that we belonged to something vaster than the present historical moment, that we were linked to centuries of Jewish wisdom and courage, weakness and strength, victory and defeat. David and Solomon, Esther, Rachel, Daniel, and Ruth were not so much models to be emulated as they were reflections of our own power and fragility, of our pride and vulnerability in being Jews in a hostile world. We compared Hitler to Antiochus Epiphanes. But where were our Maccabees? Where was our Bar-Kochba? We compared the hordes of the SS to the marauding Roman soldiers. Would we have our Masada?

Some time in the summer of 1938, the government issued a new decree against Jews to set them apart from non-Jews. We knew only one reason for this measure: to make us easier targets for arbitrary and unpredictable reprisals. A new law, effective January 1, 1939, decreed that Jews would have to carry identification cards marked with a "J" in front and on the inside. I would be Rita Sara Kuhn after January first, my father explained to me, and he would be Fritz Israel Kuhn.

"I will not add Sara after my first name," I burst out. "I'm frightened... What does it mean?"

My father looked at me a long time before he answered, like someone waiting for the storm to pass. "Don't worry, Rita. Israel in Hebrew means '*Gotteskämpfer,*' (striving with God) and Sara means 'princess.' And remember, you are a princess."

He related the stories from Genesis where these names occur, and derided the ignorance of those who had honored us thus unwittingly with such illustrious names.

———

November 10, 1938 was a gray and wintry day. The sky, veiled in somber shades, like a widow in mourning, brooded darkly over the sleeping city. The air seemed studded with tears that clung to my skin as I stepped outside for my long walk to school, fourteen blocks from home.

I set out as usual that day and at first noticed nothing out of the ordinary, nothing in the first four blocks which would prepare me for the scenes I was to encounter on that morning of horrors. If the gray sky held any portents or the icy air carried any message, I was unable to decipher them.

The night of November ninth through which I had slept peacefully, had given birth to a nocturnal monster of unimaginable destructiveness. Its savage work met my eyes as soon as I turned into Kantstrasse, a main street lined with stores on both sides, many of them owned by Jews. On this street, named after the philosopher of pure Reason, the Irrational had exercised its power in an uncontrollable paroxysm of rage.

Almost instantly and without warning, I came face to face with a frightful sight. To my right and left, I saw ugly slogans scrawled on what was left of the windows of Jewish stores. So much broken glass lay scattered on the sidewalks that I had trouble not stepping on it. Merchandise, soiled and torn, lay piled in irreverent heaps on the street like yesterday's refuse. In vain I tried to avoid stepping on things that no longer seemed just objects but shreds ripped from the living fabric of human lives.

The inside of the stores looked like gaping wounds left to rot.

I was afraid to look for fear of looking at death.

Who could have done all this? And why?

My mind rejected the obvious and fearful truth; it refused to make the inevitable connection to the men in the brown uniforms and the black boots that my father had first warned us about and whom I had since seen parading in the streets of my city with their raucous songs and cries of "*Sieg Heil.*"

Not many people were out that morning. It felt as though I were walking through a graveyard. Nothing I had ever experienced, read or heard about in the ten years of my life could help me now believe that what I was looking at was done by human hands. No legends of super giants, no fairy tales of wicked witches that had peopled my childish imagination could possibly equal this eruption of human furor and revenge.

As I walked on and saw scene after scene of destruction, of senseless violence done to material goods, it began to feel like a personal violation. The Star of David, the word "*Jude*" scrawled in red paint that dripped like blood, was meant for me too. I sensed this instantly. What my eyes were seeing and my mind could no longer reject was the awful knowledge that I was no longer just a spectator of the destruction before me, but one of its targets. Almost instinctively, I hid the necklace with the small silver Star of David my parents had given me as an initiation present for starting at a Jewish school. It felt safer to have it next to my skin.

I did not run. For where could I run without meeting the perpetrators? The giant enemy had as yet no face, though I felt his presence everywhere - inside the ravaged stores, stalking behind, or jumping at me unexpectedly from closed doors. There must have been hordes of them to have done so much damage in a single night. Years of accumulated, barely suppressed hatred had spilled into the streets unimpeded, like pus from a festering wound.

I continued walking, hoping to reach my school, a place always associated in my mind with warmth and safety. Before I reached Fasanenstrasse, I saw two of my classmates walking towards me and, recognizing me, they waved their arms in a gesture that meant not to go any further. I stopped, waiting for them with growing apprehension. The look on their faces, their eyes wide with incredulity and shock, their mouths open as if ready for a scream prepared me to expect the worst. In hushed but agitated voices they told me what was indeed the worst.

"Our synagogue is burning. The whole building is in flames... our school too."

"Our synagogue is burning?" I repeated, more of a question than a statement. "How did it...? Who...?" I did not finish the question, for I knew the answer already. As though coming from a distance, I heard them talk about scores of SA and police keeping people and fire trucks away from the burning buildings: a charred ruin was all that was to be left of this magnificent temple where I, as a small child, had seen my father carry the Torah scroll on *Simchat Torah*. All valuable objects, my friends informed me, had been carried out and confiscated by troops of SA men. The sacred objects, touched and blessed by Jews for generations, were now to serve the Nazi's lust for gold and silver, irrespective of their provenance.

The Fall of the Second Temple reenacted right here, in Berlin, in the sight of all, for all the world to know.

The enormity of it had not quite penetrated the deeper layers of my consciousness. Questions surfaced instead. What kind of people would commit such sacrilege? How many must it have taken to perpetrate so much devastation? Where in the human soul do such dark and violent passions have their hiding place? And why do they erupt under cover of night and vent their fury on holy treasures? My synagogue burning... why?

I had no control over what happened next. The overwhelming urge to let people know the incomprehensible, to share with them my indignation and, perhaps, to awaken a spark of concern in them for what was being done to their fellow citizens, canceled out all other considerations.

"Our synagogue is burning! Our synagogue is burning!" I screamed, unashamed of the tears rolling down my cheeks and, turning to face passersby, I pointed to Fasanenstrasse.

My words evoked no response in those nearest me, neither of sympathy nor of derision. With faces unmoved, they met my outrage with silence. I could not tell what they may have felt. Discomfort or acquiescence? Shame or satisfaction? Their silence felt synonymous with indifference.

On this gray and cold November morning, my childhood came to an end and I was hurled into the adult world of pain and terror. That day as well was the beginning of the Shoah.

The unexpected outpouring of my anger did little to diminish my fear. On the contrary; I hardly knew where to turn next, though I knew I must go home. My classmates had gone their separate ways and I was left alone. At every step, fear of the perpetrators suddenly emerging from out of the shattered stores followed me. I sensed danger lurking in every house and every street corner I passed. Invisible though it was, the presence of evil was palpable. I wished I were as invisible as it was. I felt branded, robbed, broken, like the stores I passed. The way home seemed endless.

When I arrived home hours earlier than expected and quite distraught, my mother's expression was one of alarm rather than surprise. I tried to answer her questions, but the sentences came out in broken fragments. "Windows smashed... red paint all over... synagogue on fire... our school burning too..." The tangle of words was an apt reflection of my mental landscape, crowded with the broken images of the scenes I had twice passed through.

My mother went from being baffled to being petrified, her shock increasing as she pieced together the shreds of my narrative. She put her arm around my shoulder, spoke soothingly and finally succeeded in calming me down. I told her from beginning to end the events of the last hour. After I finished, all she could say was, "Oh my God, where are Papa and Hans?"

Now it was my turn to calm her fears. I told her that I had seen no evidence of violence done to people, only to their property. Nevertheless, she was nervous and preoccupied, struggling with thoughts she was trying to hide from me. Whatever premonitions surfaced in her after I had given her a full account of what I had seen and felt, we were both left with a taste of things to come.

What I could not know then as a factual reality became eventually a forbidding truth: the silence I encountered would enshroud Jewish lives as long as the black boots were allowed to claim the streets of Europe; the personal isolation I felt when faced with the mute reactions of my fellow Berliners was a foreshadowing of the isolation of European Jewry in the world community; the broken glass I had stepped on was a prelude to the millions of broken lives the Third Reich would claim in its insatiable hunger for power; the burning synagogues all over Germany were the precursors of the burning ovens of the death camps.

There were few opportunities for my parents to have private conversations in our limited living space, except after we had gone to bed. They had tried to hide the stark truth of Hitler's war against Jews as much as possible from their children, but when the aftershocks of November ninth had somewhat subsided in the Jewish community, they could no longer avoid speaking openly about what followed that night.

Scattered bits of information flew around our ears. My fear that I was looking at death when I saw the gaping holes of the ransacked stores was substantiated by reports that many Jews had fallen prey to the fury of the SA and were killed either in their stores or their apartments. Later on, we learned that 30,000 men had been deported to the labor camps of Dachau or Sachsenhausen, from which many never returned. Those who were released had to leave the country within 48 hours. My father spoke to us about his helping them meet the deadline of their hasty departures from Germany and from their families. He spoke about them in whispers and shielded us from the most fearsome details, though some leaked out when he was telling my mother what he had observed. Thus we learned that those who had been released after several weeks in the camps carried with them the marks of beatings on their faces or hands and the results of malnutrition on their emaciated bodies. Others suffered severe bouts of depression or mental incoherence when their thoughts would suddenly wander off to the days of their confinement, about which they had been forbidden to speak.

The Nazis issued an order for an act of propitiation in the amount of one billion Reichsmark, to be paid *by* Jews for the damage done *to* Jewish property. No word about lost Jewish lives. A cruel joke; but no one was laughing.

We were soon to learn that the beast of the night of November ninth had not been satiated with the destruction it left in its wake. The night of November ninth had merely whetted its appetite for more Jewish blood.

There had been no public outcries from the world community. World-wide silence was interpreted by the Nazis as tacit consent to the night of devastation. Hitler's "War against Jews" could thus proceed without impediment.

Many among us reacted swiftly by leaving Germany for safer shores. My father's responsibility in the Department of Emigration increased and bolstered his self-esteem as well as our hope that one day he could help his own family. In those days of Jewish powerlessness, I saw my father endowed with a special gift.

Days after the lootings, the murders, and the burning of synagogues, more laws were passed which prohibited Jews, along with dogs, from visiting public places of entertainment, restaurants, and parks. Yellow benches were provided, "*Nur für Juden,*" (for Jews only). They remained vacant.

A mass exodus of Jews from Berlin began in earnest soon after the streets had been swept clean of broken glass. My father came home every day with stories told to him by doctors, lawyers, artists, and university professors of how their careers were finished, that they would have to start anew in countries that were opening their doors. The gifts my father brought home attested to their gratitude for his efforts and success in securing them visas for emigration.

The day a law was passed barring Jewish children from attending German schools, my father decided to tell us the real reason why he had decided to transfer us to the school in Fasanenstrasse, now a charred ruin.

"It was not entirely my decision to take you out of the school on Hebbelstrasse," he explained. The principal had called him in for a conference and stated in no uncertain terms that he wanted us removed from his school because he could no longer withstand the pressure of keeping it *Judenrein.* My father had to act promptly and diplomatically so as not to frighten us with the grim truth.

The thought that he might be harboring other unpleasant truths swept through my mind like a cold draft.

———

The Nazi serpent injected its poison into the consciousness of Berliners regardless of age, social class, or intellectual endowments. Those it held in its coils had their spines crushed and their wills broken. Among the many casualties of Nazi propaganda was my cousin Klaus who was fourteen at the time, two years older than I. He seemed more like an equal to me and I had always regarded him as an older brother. He attended a Gymnasium and was my model due to his love of learning. I felt both envy and admiration for his serious dedication to his studies.

Klaus grew up without his father, who had committed suicide when Klaus was two years old. The story was that he was driven to this desperate act because of financial bankruptcy, whether from gambling debts or failed business ventures was never clear to me. His wife, our Tante Liesel, raised her son while also taking over the management of my grandmother's store, whose progressive ailment of varicose veins eventually confined her to her wheelchair. The only male figures in Klaus's life were either from the immediate family or the occasional male friends of his mother. Our maternal grandfather could hardly be counted as a male model for someone with Klaus's mental alacrity and drive, although they were living under the same roof. He was essentially a fatherless child growing up in a male-dominated society that espoused the ancient Germanic code of honor and valor. The inheritors of this tradition were now the self-appointed guardians of manly virtues and grandiosity. What they preached was especially intoxicating to young and impressionable minds. Klaus, to my great dismay, succumbed.

Since Klaus never had any siblings, he and I grew up like brother and sister. Pictures taken of us before and shortly after Hans's birth bear witness to our close family resemblance and intimacy. All that began to change when he fell under the spell of the infectious speeches and songs the Nazis trumpeted everywhere. More and more, Klaus felt drawn to swear unquestioning allegiance to the *Führer* he admired. He seemed like one mesmerized and, with apparent innocence, mimicked the slogans and justifications for what the Nazis did at home and abroad for the greater glory of the Third Reich. He subscribed to all of it with youthful ardor and, as far as I could determine, with a deliberate turning away from the bitter truths of the regime he supported.

Klaus's growing infatuation with National Socialism left me angry and bewildered when I saw him supplanting the innocence of our childhood with the corrupt politics of our adversaries. He did not, it must be said, embrace the virulent anti-Semitism of his leaders. The overt and vicious persecution of Jews could not escape his awareness, but he was too enamored with the new Germany to take a stand against it. In that he was like the majority of Germans who defended their allegiance to the *Führer* with the argument that he was good for the German people, especially those who had suffered years of unemployment and deprivation.

My parents had tried to keep the menace of the outside world from their children's lives, and now it invaded us from within the family itself. I felt enraged, betrayed, and saddened by my cousin's blind conversion to Nazi ideology and needed to express my disaffection with him in some way. I needed to reassert the old trust and solidarity that was once ours in the Eden of our childhood.

On a day when my mother went to help her sister in the store, I decided to have a talk with Klaus. My plan was to ignore the barrier his intoxication with National Socialism had created and attempt to cure him of his blindness before he fell prey to a greater crime.

Klaus and I are sitting in his living room, playing a game of cards with popular music on the radio. Suddenly, the program is interrupted by a news announcement of major importance to the Reich. The news always followed the same line: lies upon lies about Germans being the victims of atrocities in countries outside Germany; hence the need for a greater Germany. This time the news is more frightening. Troops are mobilizing to march into Poland to avenge the atrocities committed against Germans in that country. Germans will be given ration cards in due time to provide for the build-up of the *Wehrmacht* charged with the protection of Germany and its citizens. We listen for a while to the denunciations of the enemy and of world Jewry until I can no longer contain my anger and turn to Klaus, who looks serious and intent.

"How can you believe all those lies about Polish atrocities? What about Nazi atrocities?" The words burst forth as quickly as they rush into my mind.

"What do you mean - lies?" Klaus asks in return, with obvious shock at my accusations.

"Hitler is full of lies," I continue, seeing him somewhat subdued and vulnerable. "How can you believe in a government that rules by terror and hate? And speaking of atrocities... look what he has already done to Jews in your *teures Deutschland* (beloved Germany), and will do to other nations now that there is going to be a war."

Klaus's answer is full of the usual banalities and oft-repeated slogans that assault the ear from every radio station, offend the eye from every newspaper and public poster displayed throughout the city for the education of its inhabitants. "Hitler is doing a lot of good for Germany." My cousin argues excitedly and with conviction in his voice, as though these clichés express an original thought. "He has lifted our pride again in being German; he has given us back our faith in our national and cultural greatness; he has restored for us the memory of a noble past and given us a vision for an even greater future. And, above all, he has given us jobs, a secure livelihood for families and their children. People can rest at night knowing the government will provide for them."

"Yes, by taking things away from us," I reply vehemently, "from Jews like my father, your Onkel Fritz, the husband of the aunt you love so much, who cannot rest at night for worrying about feeding her family."

The reference to my mother's hardships helps to diminish his enthusiasm somewhat. He concedes that my father's long unemployment had indeed been an unfortunate result of the new policies and that he had felt sorry for us at the time. But now he seems to find solace in the fact that my father is working again and, he emphasizes, is being employed at a job where he can help his own people. Klaus sounds convinced that many measures taken against Jews are a temporary expediency until some economic stability can be attained.

"Hitler merely intends to redistribute the opportunities for jobs among all people, to give everyone a fair chance for employment," he explains with some degree of confidence.

"That's not the point, Klaus, and you know it," I object, feeling increasingly exasperated with his facile rationalizations. I remind him that Hitler did not take Jews only from their positions as professors, doctors, lawyers, artists, and businessmen in order to give their jobs to non-Jews, but that he is now driving them out of Germany because of endless restrictions, discriminations, and *Hetzreden* (slander).

"Why does he hate us so much?" I want to know, remembering the night of November ninth. "What does he mean that we plan to ruin Germany? How can you accept his inflammatory speeches against Jews? It is wicked."

"It's not wickedness," Klaus says glumly and defensively, taken aback by my frankness. "It will pass when Germany can rest on a firm foundation."

Just as I am about to ask him how a war can contribute to that, my mother enters the room, tension written all over her face. She had no doubt overheard the last part of our conversation in which both of us had raised our voices. Without much ado, she tells me that it is time to go home to prepare for supper. Supper was not going to be for at least two hours, but I get up to join her as soon as I understand the real motive for her haste.

As soon as we reach home where no one can overhear us, she asks me, in a voice shaking with emotion, never to argue with Klaus about the political situation again.

"But he is my cousin, he will understand, he has to," I say with passion. "We grew up together, played games together, teased each other, loved each other. Once he told me, in childish innocence, that he wanted to marry me. We are - we were - like brother and sister."

"Yes, I remember those times too. Nevertheless," my mother's voice is firm, "all he understands now is what the leaders of the Hitler Youth are telling him. It's sad but true. Times have changed... times, and people with them, have changed. And don't discuss politics with Tante Liesel either."

"But she is your sister. She..." I am almost breathless with disbelief when my mother interrupts me.

"Of course, and always will be. Nothing can change that," my mother's tone can no longer disguise the despair she feels for our altered circumstances. "But she is first of all Klaus's mother and will take his side above anyone else, should she be pressured into having to make choices. Politics can divide families... politics and religion."

My mother seems so calm, so resigned to all these baffling realities, while I am seething with suppressed rage and secretly vow never to forget my argument with Klaus, an affront to everything I hold dear, such as the synagogue burning along with my school, such as friendships broken asunder because of Nazis shouting, "*Juden raus*." Can Klaus be witness to terrorist tactics and not shout with indignation? Had he too succumbed to the sickness of the soul that had spread like an epidemic throughout Germany?

Klaus and I remained on amicable terms whenever we met for family gatherings, but the rift was permanent. The tear in our family unity could not easily be mended while the world was in turmoil. I buried my resentment and distrust under a pile of common civilities and wondered whether the distance the times created between us would ever lessen. He will understand some day, I felt sure, he will no longer be able to evade the truth, because deep down there is a mountain of goodness in him that will surface again once the ideological fog has lifted.

Though I still clung to my belief in the essential goodness of each human being, as I was taught from earliest childhood on, my picture of human nature was beginning to take on darker hues. It frightened me how the power of evil could strike so many dumb with fear and sweep away others in a paroxysm of frenzied adulation and mass hysteria whenever there was a rally held by the Nazis or when Hitler spoke on the radio.

From the earliest days of my childhood, when I made my entry into the world of language and manners, I was taught to respect all people, to curtsey when saying "*Guten Tag*," and to speak gently even in disagreement, in accordance with the Proverb, "A gentle tongue is a tree of life."

My parents' brand of Judaism was steeped in humanistic values. To "Love thy neighbor as thyself" was translated into respect for oneself and others, second only to the love of God. They wanted me to pursue the path of righteousness and to shun evil. My father's reference to God as, *"der liebe Gott,"* instilled in me the belief that God is a loving God, a close friend to all of His creation, and a forgiving judge once I confessed my wrongdoing to Him. In that way I always thought of Him as almost being a part of me, of listening to me, of looking into my heart, rather than the stern, commanding *Herrgott*, watching and judging us with an austere detachment, without a personal relation to each of His creations. God, in my parents' eyes, was the source of goodness who had created in us a heart where the good and the evil impulses reside, but God also endowed us with the ability to choose freely between them, to let one or the other prevail.

Twenty days after the pogrom of November ninth, 1938, my parents gave me a *Poesie Album* for my eleventh birthday. Their verses well describe the conduct they wanted me to follow in life.

Gut zu denken, gut zu handeln,
Mit dem Menschen friedlich wandeln,
Auf der Lebensreise,
Nach Vollkommenheit zu ringen,
Und die Zeit gut hinzubringen,
Das sei deine Lebensweise.

To think and act with kindness,
To live with others in peace,
Throughout life's journey,
To strive for perfection,
To spend your time productively,
Let that be your way of life.

Zur Erinnerung an den 29 November
1938, von deinen dich liebenden Eltern.

In loving memory
from your parents.

Two years later, after many exclusionary laws had been passed against Jews, in the middle of a hateful war, and the beginnings of deportations of all the "undesirables of the State" into concentration camps, my mother reminded me that goodness alone is the sacred treasure that makes us truly human.

Du bist gut,	You are good,
Lass dich drob nicht necken.	Let no one deride you.
Du bist gut,	You are good,
Lass dich drob nicht schrecken.	Let no one frighten you.
Kostbarster Schatz	A most cherished treasure
Ist Guete nur allein.	Is goodness alone.
Waer'n alle Menschen gut,	If all human beings were good,
Wuerd's Paradies auf Erden sein.	That would be paradise on earth.

Meinem lieben Toechterchen	For my dear daughter given
gewidmet von ihrer Mutti. 1.16.1941	in steadfast love from her Mutti.

I never questioned the validity of the lessons taught me nor my parents' efforts to exemplify them, yet the night of November ninth brought me into contact with a violence I never thought possible to exist in the human heart. My encounter with Klaus, who closed his ears and eyes to the terror facing Jews and his immediate family members, colored in the darker areas of my picture of human nature and undermined my trust in its goodness.

The news of the invasion of Poland sent shock waves through many communities, especially the Jewish one. Germany was also well into a war with England and France. The daily news recorded one victory after another in tones of gloating vindictiveness and arrogant claims of German superiority, which some received with frenetic jubilation and others with suppressed skepticism. The mood among Jews was grim once the borders were tightened for emigration. Yet my father's job at the Emigration Department of the Jewish Community Council continued until 1941. Those with money and connections still found ways of legally getting out of Germany, leaving behind family members and possessions.

My father's two gentile friends, our Onkel Helmut and Onkel Rudi, defied the ordinance against fraternizing with Jews and came to visit us to share their dismay with their trusted friend. Onkel Rudi, a former socialist, the most outspoken of the two, described his outrage at the avalanche of events in his usual picturesque language.

"Germans are either participants or witnesses to a drunken orgy of military iniquities (*Schandtaten*). It's only a matter of time until they wake up with a stupendous hangover from which they will not soon recover."

Whether it was his cynicism or pessimism, or some gift of prophetic vision that prompted some of his more profound assessments of the destiny governing European history, his remarks often left me deep in thought; it was like looking at the future with pictures of the past superimposed.

My father responded to him with his own metaphor, "The doors of our prison are closing, Rudi, and I cannot think of a way out of it for my family."

My twelfth birthday was not far off. It was after another boast of the German *Wehrmacht* that my parents called us one evening for a family conference. The set and serious expression on their faces bore no opposition to whatever they had concluded in private talks. My father, as usual, was the first to start the conversation.

"Mama and I have been thinking and talking together a great deal about a matter that concerns all of us, but especially both of you."

I recognized the tone in his voice as bearing dire news.

"You know that Mama was born a Lutheran, don't you?"

Hans and I nodded in agreement, wondering what was to follow this introduction. My father's next question was bewildering. "Do you know about the Nuremberg Laws of 1935 to protect the purity of German blood?"

We answered in the negative. What did the phrase "purity of German blood" mean? My father simplified what he knew by explaining that, in accordance with these laws, my parents' marriage was considered a *Misch-ehe*, a mixed marriage, and that Hans and I, the offspring of such a marriage, fell into the category of *Geltungsjuden*, Jews by law, since we were all, including my "Aryan" mother, registered Jews before 1935. Her "Aryan" status, he said, was determined by her blood, "uncontaminated" by Jewish blood for generations. Her conversion to Judaism did not weigh as heavily in the balance of these laws as being born a Jew. The Nuremberg Laws regarded religion as extraneous to the more fundamental issue of race, determined by blood. In that, the Nazis represented a unique phenomenon in Jewish history, since Jews in the past could save their lives by conversion. After 1935, any co-mingling between members of the "Aryan" and members of the Jewish race was considered *Rassenschande*, pollution of the race, and was subject to punishment. Because my parents were married ten years before the Nuremberg laws went into effect, my mother's defilement of her "Aryan" blood was considered an offense rather than a crime or, as my father declared, she was, *eine edle Sünderin*, a noble sinner.

We sat in silence for some time to absorb the intricacies of these laws and to try to gauge their possible effect on our situation. My father continued.

"You know…" he began, then stopped to find the right words. "You know that we are living in grave times, and grave times call for grave decisions."

Before he related their decision to us, he used another preamble to justify it. He reminded us of the fact that anti-Semitism had always been a major element in Jewish history, that since the fall of the Second Temple, Jews had been living in the diaspora, in adopted countries that tolerated their presence, often with limited rights, often in isolation from the non-Jewish population and, in extreme cases, tolerated them only after they had converted to Christianity, forced upon them under threat of death. Hitler, he concluded, was one of a long line of persecutors, though he may well be the most venomous and fanatical one. He could no longer shield us from this bitter truth, though he hoped to protect us from coming perils.

"We don't know how severe the measures against Jews will be, but to live with false hopes, we believe, is suicidal. Since all escape routes are closed to us, we thought of a plan that might yet protect you."

He paused again, looking at us to see our reaction to these preparatory remarks of what he was going to tell us next. "Mama and I think your status as *Geltungsjuden* may change if you change your religious status, that is, if you let yourselves be baptized."

My first impulse was to voice my objection immediately with an emphatic "No." Instead, I reminded him that it was race, or blood, not religion that determined one's status in the Germany of Hitler, and that our status had already been decided long before 1935. My father conceded that point, admitting that their plan was a desperate effort to save us from further persecution, that it might not work, but that it was worth the gamble.

My parents and I argued back and forth. The more I sensed their determination to clutch at this last means to spare their children whatever fate was awaiting Jews, the more obstinately I rejected their proposal. I thought of other members of my Jewish family, I thought of all my friends for whom there was no way out of the perilous trap. I did not want to think of myself as a traitor, a coward, by adopting the faith of our enemies.

"I won't do it... Never..." My voice broke with anger and the fear of entering into open conflict with my parents. The rock of resistance stuck in my throat. My father noticed the struggle in me and surprised me with his response. His voice was calm and gentle, expressing a certain pride in my insurrection when he turned to me directly.

"I understand, *Püppchen*... truly, I do. I know God will also understand..."

"No, He won't," I interrupted him, feeling as sure as I have ever been of anything. Encouraged by my father's compassionate tone, I reiterated my argument. "He will not forgive me for adopting the faith of the enemy who intends to destroy our people. You have raised me in the Jewish faith and, if I have to die for it, so be it. I will die as a Jew! I don't want to live because of a lie..." I stopped, overcome more with dread of God's punishment for my betrayal than fear of what the Nazis might do to me.

My father, moved by my agitation, took my hand in his with a tenderness I had seldom experienced. There was no vindictiveness, no condescension or reprimand in his voice when he spoke again, this time with less firmness and resoluteness.

"Believe me when I tell you that your mother and I have not come to this decision lightheartedly. We have weighed everything on a fine scale, and have even anticipated your objections because we share them in our hearts. Our plan may not work... we just don't know... we just don't know."

He withdrew into himself, following thoughts he was reluctant to express. His apparent anguish at seeing me struggle made me forget my own, all the more so when my mother joined the conversation to tell us of their dilemma.

"Your father is right. We did not make this decision lightheartedly or with indifference to your feelings, Rita, which we well know. Quite the contrary; we took everything into account. Besides, Rita, you must not regard all Christians as our enemies. There are a good number of Christians who remember that the cornerstone of Christianity is Judaism and abhor the anti-Semitism of the regime. Some of them have had to pay for it with their lives."

She reminded us of her own defiance of the strident anti-Semitism she was taught in her Lutheran religion classes and how she herself, a twelve-year-old at the time, had decided to renounce Christianity altogether to be able to cling to her faith in a more charitable God.

"I firmly believe that God wants us to live and not give in to the powers of darkness, but fight them in any way possible. Some goodness has to survive this madness," she concluded.

She was right, of course, but I kept on arguing. They did not argue in return but rather agreed with me on many points, insisting all the while that it was a desperate attempt and might not have the results they hoped for. My father finally felt he had to respond to my growing desperation of what was really at the center of my concern, namely the fear that God would punish me, would not forgive me.

"Listen, *Püppchen*," he said, "we are not asking you to renounce the God of Israel to whom you have prayed ever since you were a little girl. On the contrary, we are placing our lives into His hands, to do with in accordance with His will. We will keep Him in our hearts, pray to Him in the solitude and safety of our own walls, in silence, if necessary, and remember always that He delivered the children of Israel from their bondage in Egypt. If your baptism is wrong in any way, He will not spare you the fate of the other Jews. There is not the slightest chance of our ever leaving Germany... this may be the only chance to protect us from further dangers... maybe."

What my mother said next helped me to think of everything in a different perspective, to reconcile myself to the inevitable.

"Don't forget, Rita, that Jesus was a Jew and prayed to the same God whom you address in your *Sh'ma*. The God of the Jews and the Christians is the same God, the only God, no matter how much people disagree on that point. Just remember, when you say your prayers, you pray to the one and only God, as the *Sh'ma* tells us."

The last remnant of my resistance was thus broken, though my fear of divine judgment remained. As soon as I was alone in our room, one phrase resounded in my mind with such insistence that I spoke aloud the words over and over again, "Dear God... do not spare me... do not spare me."

Our religion lessons in the New Testament took place in the Trinitatis Kirche at Karl August Platz. The New Testament had been a sealed book to us thus far. Now, each Sunday morning, Hans and I listened to the Reverend Dr. Becker reveal to us the story of Jesus, his miraculous birth, his mission for which he was predestined, his teachings, and his sufferings until his death on the cross. We were eager listeners, Hans and I, though I read the Gospels with detached curiosity, my inner resistance still standing as a barrier to the real meaning behind the words. An instantaneous rejection of the Virgin birth, prompted by natural reasoning, blinded me at first to the more credible aspects of the man Jesus. The numinous quality of his words, the vivid and penetrating imagery of his parables, his loving concern for the poor and the oppressed, all raised in me an empathetic interest. He spoke to me in strange and inexplicable ways, as though a long-forgotten voice, a hidden truth, had found new life in me. I started to listen more with my heart than with my ears alone and soon discovered a continuity with Jewish thought I had been taught in Hebrew lessons, though carried to a more mystical dimension.

Nevertheless, during our reading of the Gospels, I often felt like a trespasser, walking into a gathering of the faithful, and feared I might be expelled any moment. I was, after all, an imposter, having no intention of becoming a true convert. I was driven to this place by expediency and not by faith. I felt close to the Jew in Jesus, his affinity to the teachings of the Bible, and resented the exclusiveness of religious doctrine, resented the rift, the hate between Christians and Jews that had given rise to so many persecutions and pogroms of Jews throughout the centuries.

Perhaps I wanted to feel less like a traitor to all my Jewish friends and compatriots when I recognized in Jesus a wise Jew of great virtue, a Rabbi, a teacher of moral excellence, however remote from us in his holiness. From Hebrew school I remembered admonishments to make our lives holy, to follow the path of righteousness and compassion, and I embraced Jesus as one of us, persecuted for his faith in the God of Israel, his love for the prophets of the Bible whose path he followed, and his staunch advocacy for those in need. He wanted to remind an ailing world of its spiritual roots, a world that seemed much like ours, torn with dissension, corruption, and moaning under the burden of ruthless oppression. The integrity of his mission and his courage in laying it before the world without regard to his own advantage or safety made me feel the misery of our own times all the more keenly. I compared him to those who spoke out against the evil of our time and were willing to risk their lives, and I knew that the persecution of the brave and the good would continue.

Jesus, Reverend Becker told us, was the Messiah, a concept that contradicted my religious instructions in Hebrew school where I was taught that the Messiah will not come to a world that has strayed from God, where wickedness is rampant, and human beings place their own power above that of God. The Messiah, on the contrary, will come to a world united to strive after righteousness of its own volition, in purity of heart and devotion to the study of Torah. If Jesus, as the Messiah, wanted to unite all people in his "Father's mansions," then why was there such a schism amongst the believers, leading to wars and persecutions?

These questions surfaced during our lessons with Dr. Becker. Nonetheless, that did not prevent me from being wholly absorbed in the readings of the New Testament. The teachings of Jesus, the Rabbi, struck me often as a breath of warmth come into a cold room. Yet I was always led back to the God of Judaism, to whom I had turned ever since I learned to pray and who needed no human intercessor.

I needed to believe in the God of my childhood; I needed that intimate connection with my awesome Friend; I needed to believe that my life had value in His eyes or it would dry up like bones in the desert sun.

It was early one morning when, all alone, I battled my way against the icy wind to arrive on time at the Trinitatis Kirche for my religious lessons. The air seemed studded with darts of cold thrown by an invisible archer against whom there was little protection in this season of arctic temperatures. The sidewalks were covered with a thin layer of ice and I imagined myself walking on the sharp blade of a sword that was cutting through my defenses against the shame and guilt I felt for these early morning trespasses into forbidden territory.

The deserted streets only enhanced my sense of isolation and secrecy whenever thoughts of November ninth returned to remind me of my first spiritual home, now a charred skeleton. These thoughts clashed painfully with my present intent and the temptation to retrace my steps, to confront my parents with the burdensome nature of their request, slowed down my steps and I engaged in an imaginary dialogue with them. I wanted to tell them that I felt like a traitor, that the fear of detection never left me, and that I could not look my friends straight in the eyes anymore. I was as much afraid of human as I was of divine judgment. My parents would have to relieve me of this contract.

With these thoughts in mind, I did not notice the dark figure of a man standing near the curb of the street I was about to cross until I was only a few feet away from him. He seemed to have appeared out of nowhere. He was looking at me directly, smiling, as though he had expected me. As I approached the curb, he opened his heavy winter coat and exposed himself to me, his hand playing with his member in an inviting gesture, as if offering me a toy. I froze, looked in disbelief first and then in horror. He beckoned me to come closer when a sudden flash of understanding freed me to run for safety. My punishment flashed through my mind as I hastened to the church as to a protective sanctuary.

That we were not wanted anywhere was made abundantly clear by strategically placed, hard to ignore signs which read in formal German, "*Juden hier nicht erwünscht*," (Jews not wanted here) or, in more legalistic language, "*Zutritt für Juden verboten*" (Admittance to Jews prohibited). They met our eyes from a variety of public places.

The world for us was becoming a cage.

Prohibitions hit home, literally, when Jews were no longer allowed to rent apartments in houses owned by "Aryans." They were to move into so-called *Judenhäuser*, houses either owned by Jews or chosen by the state for Jewish tenants only. Our notice of eviction came a few months after the ordinance was first made public in 1939.

"The owner of our house is of pure German blood," my father informed us in a derisive tone one day, "and we must not contaminate his property with our Jewish presence. We have to move in less than a month."

Panic followed his announcement. How were we going to find an apartment in one of those *Judenhäuser* in less than a month? Our family was one of many rushing to find a house designated by these laws as fit only for Jews.

My father theorized that this was another measure to isolate us further from the non-Jewish population, to create, so to speak, an invisible ghetto. The thought that this policy would also make it easier for the Gestapo to capture Jews was never mentioned among us.

We had almost given up hope when my mother, like a winged messenger, came home one day bearing good news. A customer in my aunt's store had heard that an apartment was available in the very house where our two aunts had lived before moving to Biesdorf. It was two houses away from my grandmother's store and had a Jewish owner who had emigrated to America. The people living there now wanted to move to another apartment in the same housing complex because they did not want to share their living space with a Jewish co-tenant, a Frau Philipps. Our new address would be Sybelstrasse 62.

The prospect of living so close to my mother's family was a turn of events we scarcely thought possible. It was like the sight of land to a shipwrecked crew.

When we at last had the keys to the apartment in our hands, we wanted to see in it a particularly favorable omen. There were other advantages to our move as well. Our new living quarters were part of a larger apartment that had belonged to the above mentioned Frau Philipps, a widow in her eighties. She had to relinquish four of the five rooms to make space for other tenants. She herself occupied one of the larger front rooms. Another large front room was occupied by Frau Schmidt, a gentile woman, who had no objections to sharing an apartment with Jews. We were to occupy the other three rooms, one of them a spacious "Berliner Zimmer" (parlor), and two smaller bedrooms, one of which we had to give up later to another Jewish tenant. We had our own bathroom but had to share the kitchen with the other tenants.

Frau Philipps was an enigma to all of us. She talked little and spent most of the time in her room, packed to full capacity with what was left of her furniture. From the small opening of her door, we could see there were large, heavy, and dark pieces of furniture, one against the other, that left just enough space for her to walk but less for the sunlight to penetrate the gloomy darkness. It was like the burial chamber of a high official of an ancient court whose earthly goods would accompany her on the journey to the beyond. Frau Philipp's only link to the living was feeding the birds that swarmed to her balcony and to her generous donations of stale bread crumbs. They left their calling cards all over the balcony as evidence of her generosity long after her supply had ceased. The only time she ventured out of her cave was at mealtime. Then we could hear her shuffling walk through the front hall and could see her back bent over the stove or the sink, her body covered with black, shapeless garments, her shoulders stooped over, looking not unlike the illustrations of witches from my childhood storybooks.

Frau Schmidt was the exact opposite. As if to compensate for our gloomy co-tenant, she spread cheerfulness all around, never at a loss for words, smiles, or male companions, even though she was a married woman. Her husband, Arno, had been drafted early on to fight *diesen wahnsinnigen Krieg* (this crazy war) for the Fatherland, rather unwillingly it must be said. She gave us easy access to her room, large, bright, and tastefully furnished, where we could listen to the radio and where I was allowed to explore her small but well-chosen library of German classics and other books from around the world. It was a gold mine of discovery, an opening to the world of ideas, where I first met Shakespeare, Tolstoy, Dostoyevsky, Hugo, and many more, all ready food for my insatiable appetite for reading.

After we were settled in our new home, my father leaned back in his armchair one evening and, satisfied with food and our extraordinary good luck, he said contentedly, "*Der liebe Gott hat's diesmal gut mit uns gemeint,*" (Our dear God has been favorable to us this time).

"This time," I thought to myself, doubtful whether God had anything at all to do with it. I was beginning to question His involvement with human affairs, though I was not ready yet to allow a sense of abandonment to enter my thinking.

Chapter 3

In the Howling Storm - Mira

O Rose, thou art sick,
The invisible worm
That flies in the night,
In the howling storm

Has found out thy bed
Of crimson joy,
And his dark secret love
Does thy life destroy.

—WILLIAM BLAKE, *"The Sick Rose"*

Wahnsinn, Wahnsinn, (madness) was the favorite word one of my father's gentile friends used to comment on the political situation whenever he and his wife came for a visit to give us the latest news. *Wahnsinn* was a word on the lips of any clear-thinking person, and was meant to describe a multitude of incidents and the people causing them, from the air raids by the British bombers to the Gestapo raids on Jews and suspected enemies of the Reich. My father's friend, Rudolf Konzca, was most vocal on the subject of madness "roaming the streets, the highways, the airways, the villages, the forests of Europe, leaving its ugly marks for generations to come." He spoke, almost prophetically, of Germany having to bear the mark of Cain for future ages as a warning; that nations would forget this was once the land of Lessing, of Goethe and Schiller, of Bach and Beethoven, and would remember only Hitler and Himmler, the reincarnations of the hydra of Greek mythology. He would conclude these outbursts of indignation by saying, "I blush for every decent German."

Rudolf Konzca, whom Hans and I called "Onkel Rudi," was my father's bookish friend who loved to quote from his copious reading of old and new writers, among them his favorite, Joseph Conrad, whom he suggested I should read as though I were already an adult. He loved to fill our ears with his utopian dreams of a free society to which he clung with obstinate fervor, remnants of the days when he was an active member of the Socialist Party, which, he lamented, should have won the elections instead of the "little corporal," Adolf Hitler, whom he despised as much as he loved his Schiller. He was my father's most voluble friend. He always came with his wife Maria, who said very little but would just smile at him in deferential silence and with unabashed pride. The rest of us, too, would listen to the words gushing out of him as soon as he found himself in the safe company of trusted friends, as if a dam had broken loose.

Whether it was my age or his verbal effusiveness, there were times I had trouble following his words, punctuated with literary allusions and quotations from a wide array of writers. I began to think of him as being a rather wild eccentric, an undisciplined bibliophile with a kind and loyal heart, though embittered by the ugly visage of evil showing itself everywhere and mocking his idealism. I felt some pity for him and his unappeased need for a free and uncensored exchange of ideas that filled his mind to the bursting point. He was like one who had inherited goods for which the world had no longer any use. I felt akin to him for his love for books, but also like a stranger to his often rambling discourse. His loyalty to my father was his most endearing quality.

"*Tja*, Rudi," my father would interrupt his friend's nostalgic reminiscences of happier times, "your dream and Hitler's megalomania are poles apart. I heard the news on Frau Schmidt's radio last night, followed by Hitler's speech, and I almost soiled my pants from fright."

We had received with mounting fear the news of the occupation of Norway, Belgium, Holland, and of the easy surrender of France. Hitler had raved ecstatically about the vistas opening up for his realization of the Thousand Year Reich. People had cheered and lent their voice to his grandiose scheme. It was terrifying.

"Ah yes, the masses," Uncle Rudi responded with a sigh at the mention of the gullibility of so many Germans. His voice took on a wistful and bitter tone. He reminded us that he had once spoken for them, rallied to their defense, fought for their rights, and had felt close to those poor, downtrodden, long-suffering, and inarticulate masses, those multitudes of the oppressed who willingly turned oppressor at the mere wink from their *Fuhrer*. They had been like family to Rudi, but now they looked to him like so many *Hampelmänner* (puppet), who moved into action only when someone pulled their strings, and the one pulling was Dr. Goebbels, that pseudo-intellectual *mit nem Klotzfuss*, (with a big clubfoot). Rudi agreed with my father how frightening it was to think of the many spongy brains ready to soak up any rubbish fed to them by the little Minister of Propaganda with his extremely skillful verbal manipulation. Rudi was not impressed, but dismissed him with a shrug, "Hollow rhetoric to hollow people... hollow, but extremely dangerous."

I loved these visits of Rudi and Maria, who continued them despite the ban on fraternizing with Jews by non-Jews, and who thereby risked arrest or worse. Another gentile friend of my father's, "Uncle" Helmut, also took that risk and spent many evenings with us, playing a game of cards, *Skat*, with my father or "Rummy" with all of us. Helmut was the opposite of Rudi; he was a quiet, well-spoken, handsome man with refined manners, whose warm interest in us personally and as a family often revived our flagging spirits and faith in human nature. Helmut was the head-waiter in one of the best hotels in Berlin, and related anecdotes to us about his encounters with a diversity of guests at the hotel.

One encounter in particular, which occurred when Germany was already at war with Russia, made an indelible impression on me. A young

SS man, not much more than twenty years old, had been sitting at the bar and recounted to the guests within earshot a battle in Russia in which he had lost a leg. "Serves me right," was his final comment, leaving everyone to ponder his remark.

It was on evenings such as these that all of us felt relieved of the usual fear of denunciation for talking freely in condemnation of the regime. With friends and family we found the strength to face another day, another night of terror. Friendships sustained us, sheltered us, and grounded us, though they often took on the same evanescent quality that life in Berlin had assumed for those of us who lost friends through voluntary exile or forced deportation.

There was one friendship, rare in its duration, which for four years triumphed over the vicissitudes of our situation; it was my friendship with Mira. We first met in 1939 when we attended the same school.

One day in class, a new girl is sitting next to me in a seat vacated by a girl who had left for England. The new girl introduces herself to me with a brief, "Hello. My name is Mira... Mira Holzheim." I nod and give her a smile of acknowledgement. "Hello. Mira Sara Holzheim, right? I'm Rita... Rita Sara Kuhn." We smile at each other tentatively in recognition of the recent addition to our names and continue with our lesson.

Mira has dark curly hair, brown eyes in a round face and olive-colored skin. She is somewhat chubby and you would not call her pretty, but rather pleasant looking, her gentle and unassuming manner inspiring confidence. We soon become friends outside of class as well, and visit with each other at our homes, doing homework together, gossiping about boys, classmates, or sharing the secrets of our burgeoning womanhood. She is more developed than I, has started to menstruate, and sympathizes with me when I tell her my grievances about girls calling me *Plättbrett* (ironing board), because I am still flat-chested. It is some time before I learn of her 'secret,' which is going to change our friendship in significant ways.

Early one morning, during our first class period, I happen to look at Mira and notice her mouth twitching in a way that fills me with unease, but I feel too constrained to ask for its meaning. Mira herself seems like a person far removed from her immediate surroundings. Her eyes have an inward, expectant look; her whole body, tense yet resigned, seems to be waiting for a momentous event about to happen. Suddenly she raises her hand and asks for permission to go to the nurse's office.

"Can Rita come with me?" Mira asks as she prepares to leave, much to my surprise.

"Of course," our teacher replies, drawing out the words with emphatic warmth. She must know something I don't, I wonder.

On the way to the nurse's office, Mira tells me her 'secret.' She is an epileptic, has been for some time. She gives me a brief run-down of her convulsions, beginning with the twitching of her mouth which, as I learn now, is the first sign of an oncoming attack. She is not conscious during the seizures and feels no pain, she reassures me, though it may seem so to the person watching. In all my twelve years I have never heard the word 'convulsion' and can form no image of it. Mira describes it in some detail. She gives me directions of what I am supposed to do. Seeing that I am hesitant, she reassures me again that I have nothing to fear and that she had asked that I go with her more for comfort and companionship than for help. "*Ich fühle mich dann nicht so ganz allein,* (I don't feel quite so alone then)."

As soon as we come to the nurse's office, Mira knows exactly what to do. She lies down on a narrow cot near the entrance and waits. I pull up a chair beside her and wait with her. I start a conversation to hide my nervousness. While we are making idle chatter, I keep watching her mouth and soon see the quivers increase in frequency and intensity until they spread throughout her whole body. Mira is slipping slowly into unconsciousness. There is no more talk.

Once her convulsions begin in earnest, I see Mira writhing, twisting, and straining every muscle in her body until I fear her blood vessels will surely break. The sight of her convulsed body horrifies me. I feel helpless, terrified, fascinated ... completely useless. Her eyes are closed, her face is growing rigid and turning purple with the strain. I look on in awe and pity. She seems to be under the control of some alien power, some demon invading her defenseless body to gain possession of her beleaguered soul at all costs, even her very life. This invisible enemy is fighting for ultimate supremacy and I wonder who will win. Her teeth, I find, are tightly clenched together, too tight to place a handkerchief between them, as she had instructed me earlier. The only help I can give is to keep her from falling off the narrow cot. I touch her body, feeling both revulsion and compassion. I cannot understand how her young body is able to withstand such an onslaught. How much longer before she will be freed of this wrenching struggle?

In her convulsed body, fighting some inner tyrant, I see our daily struggle against a very visible enemy trying to gain possession of our physical and spiritual existence, and I know I am bonded to Mira from this day on. Only the most extreme force will succeed in severing this tie. After about fifteen minutes, Mira slowly regains consciousness, sees that I am still there, and closes her eyes to rest.

How overwhelming the strain on her had been shows clearly after it is all over. She tries to talk but is still too weak. Her tongue is swollen from biting it during the seizure; the words come out muffled and indistinct. Several capillaries in her face are broken, leaving purplish lines running throughout her skin like branches of a tree.

Mira rallies amazingly fast from her ordeal of which she remembers little, if anything at all, but which will stay with me for as long as I live. After a while, I can make out her words which form into a question, "Were you terribly frightened?" I nod my head slightly, not wanting to tell her a lie but also not wanting to add to her discomfort by admitting how terrified I had been. I reassure her that I am alright, now that I see her well again.

To my question of whether she is in any pain, she replies that her tongue is sore, often the result of these attacks.

On our way back to the classroom, Mira extracts a promise from me that comes as no surprise. "Will you be with me whenever I have another seizure?" I give her my word, reaffirming the same pledge I had made while she was unconscious.

Another new girl enters our classroom one day and all eyes, open with amazement, are fastened on her with enough intensity to burn holes into her skin. I check my own reaction against that of my classmates to read in their faces a mirror image of my own thought: how homely she is. The smiles on the faces of my peers, heads turned close to each other in whispers and giggles, convince me that I was not alone in my response to this new addition to our class. The girl behind me comments, rather too loudly, "She looks like an ostrich." At that remark, Mira and I join the gigglers.

Seemingly unperturbed by the sudden stir her entrance has created, the new girl takes the seat assigned to her by our teacher; she is either oblivious or accustomed to the response she evokes from her peers, for it is unlikely that she cannot hear some of the remarks and suppressed snickers.

Her name is Vera F. She is unusually tall for a girl of thirteen. Her head, on an uncommonly long neck, looks disproportionately small to the rest of her body. "Her neck must've got stretched when the doctor pulled her out," the same girl behind me whispers to her neighbor. Those around her break into laughter upon hearing this derisive yet plausible explanation for that part of Vera's anatomy.

Vera reminded me of pictures I had once seen in a book in my aunt's library in Biesdorf on the history of early civilizations, which I studied with fascination. What had intrigued me particularly were several illustrations of large and small statuettes of goddesses dating as far back as 6,000 B.C.E., attesting to the worship of female deities during a period of Matriarchy. Vera resembled the representation of either a bird or a snake goddess. She had a receding chin, a pronounced Jewish nose which, she confessed to me later, had always been the bane of her existence, and small, watery blue eyes. Besides that, she was a redhead with thin hair that looked like an overused toothbrush and, as is true for many redheads, she had an abundance of freckles covering her face and arms. She moved her rather graceless body, her long arms and large hands, with the awkwardness of someone who is aware, painfully aware, of its imperfections. I looked for one redeeming feature in Vera's appearance - her mouth, her ears, her torso, any part of her - and could find none. Nature had not been very kind; not bestowing on her even the most minimal of feminine graces.

We ridicule her mercilessly behind her back, and the more ruthless among us allude to her defects in not-too-subtle ways in her presence. On a day when there is a peculiar odor in the classroom, whether its source came from the recent air raid or it had some other cause, we all start commenting on it. I overhear one girl remark to Vera, "*Ach, du Arme*, you must be able to smell it twice as much," a rude reference to Vera's large nose. I feel resentment at the girl's crudity, but keep silent.

For a long time we exclude Vera from our games, our conversations, our confidences, and do not invite her to our homes. To compensate for her rejection by her peers, Vera uses her natural mental endowments, which are considerable, to impress her teachers with her fine performances in almost every subject. This invariably earns her the approval of teachers but increases our scorn all the more.

The taunts of my classmates, meeting with no resistance from Vera or the teachers, become so vicious that Mira and I feel ashamed and sorry for the recipient of so much abuse. We begin to question our complicity with her tormentors and gradually start to separate ourselves from them. The cruel paradox of our treatment of Vera impresses us with such force that we decide to act on our misgivings. Mira, not surprisingly, feels a special affinity with Vera, since she herself had often experienced exclusion from

the circle of her peers because of her epilepsy, which frightens and alien-
ates some children. Sometimes, Mira confided once, she feels like a leper
among healthy people.

Why was it then that human beings like us, caricatured, slandered,
ghettoized, and abused for hundreds of years, could find such satisfaction
in ostracizing one of our own merely because she fell short of the standard
of attractiveness? Was it the petty arrogance alone of teenage girls whose
values are largely determined by external appearance and social graces that
prompted us in our ridicule of Vera? Or was it because we saw in her the
reflection of every caricature of the Jew, from the *Stürmer* on down, the
stereotypical Jew with the hated Semitic features exaggerated to grotesque
proportions, the chinless face, the sensual lips, the large hooked nose?
Were we trying to repudiate these offensive distortions of our people by
repudiating Vera who was a faint replica of them?

Who was Vera? Vera the person? What was hiding beneath her homely
exterior? How did she feel about herself? About us? I had to find out.

One day Vera and I board the same compartment of the train going
home. At first we speak hesitantly to each other, but soon discover things
we have in common. We live within walking distance from each other;
she has two brothers with whom she has squabbles similar to mine with
my brother. Our taste in literature coincides somewhat, whether it is the
poetry of Heine and Goethe, or the novels of Stefan Zweig, Hermann
Hesse and Dostoyevsky. We both enjoy reading Shakespeare in translation.
Our parents have, however, different backgrounds; her father used to be
a prominent lawyer, whom even the Nazis acknowledged by giving him a
prestigious job in the *Jüdische Gemeinde*. Her mother had gone to the university for a while before her marriage, and afterward helped her husband
in the office. By the time we get off the train and say *Auf Wiedersehen*, we
agree to get together some time after school at one of our homes.

I feel a little closer to the real Vera already.

Yet, the next day, when we are together in the classroom and Vera wants to resume our contact, I hesitate, look around the class, uncertain of how my classmates will react to my new friendship. Vera seems to understand that I am not quite ready to go against the trend and she lets me be. More than ever I feel shame, but admire the dignity with which she handles my betrayal. At this moment, I think of her as being vastly superior to our pettiness.

We continue this charade for a while longer, restricting our friendship to after school hours until the farce sickens me enough and I decide, to hell with the others, and act as naturally in class with Vera as I do outside of it. The snickering remarks cease altogether once my peers accept Vera's inclusion in my circle of friends.

From Mira and Vera I learned the meaning of friendship in ways I did not fully understand until later, but one thing was clear: we were all outcasts, regardless of appearance, character, or social class. Despite our differences, that was our bond. The hours of laughter we shared as well as the moments of anguish provided us with the armor we needed for the struggles ahead.

In the evenings, we gathered around the large dining-room table and talked. My mother's collection of crystal on the large sideboard glistened as usual like distant stars, happy reminders of days gone by. There stood the tall wine flasks, the large serving platter and bowl, and wine glasses large and small, all of them no longer in use. To me they were beacons of light in a darkening world.

My father loved to tell us stories of yesterday, before anyone had even known of a Hitler, and we imagined what life might have been like if Hitler had never been allowed to leave his prison cell. We might be living in a house large enough for four people, surrounded by trees and with ample space for a small garden. We would have a car and enough to eat but, above all, we would be free from fear.

My mother drew comfort from recalling the many times her young husband-to-be took her to the opera, the symphony, or the theater; or the outings in my father's small French sports car. She would take out later pictures of him sitting in the back of his Pierce Arrow with the chauffeur posing in front, or of both of them with their caps and goggles on, standing at the door of his sports car and smiling in anticipation of the trip ahead.

"*Ach ja, die Symphonie,*" my father sighed at the mention of the word.

As a young man he was wont to bring a musical score to the symphony ever since he had become fluent in reading music. He used it at concerts to follow the music and judge the conductor's interpretation of it. He had plans of becoming a composer and conductor of his own compositions, and could claim several of his own when still young. His father, however, discouraged him in that endeavor and held out quite a different career for his only son and heir, urging him to follow family tradition and become a banker. My grandfather prevailed and my father became successful in the banking business but, he assured us, his heart was elsewhere.

"Tell them of the time you registered in the Conservatory and came home to tell your parents," my mother prodded, never tired of hearing that story.

"I was about seventeen at the time," my father began his reminiscence. "All I ever wanted to do then was to study and play music. Music was my life, my daily food."

He had started to play the piano as background music for silent films, *der Übung halber* (for the sake of practice), but he wanted to follow his dream and give it reality. His first step was to go to the Conservatory and register there. When he came home to tell his parents, his announcement was greeted with stunned silence. The father gave his son one long hard look and, as was his manner, gently but definitively asked him to go back the same day and cancel his registration, giving him only one reason: he did not want his son to become a *Hungerkünstler* (a starving artist). My father's admiration of the grandfather I knew only from hearsay (he died before I was two years old), was true also of his devotion to his mother.

He trusted their judgment to work in his favor and so he went back to the Conservatory to carry out his father's request.

After all these years and despite the enforced change of career, my father never ceased to express his gratitude toward his father for guarding him against possible failure. But on that day, he readily admitted, he had felt resentment for having to say good-bye to his dream, though never to his love of music.

Hans and I listened to these stories from the past and I tried to see in the father before me the seventeen-year-old, burning with his one passion, with wild romantic dreams, such as I knew the great composers to have had. And then the young man, tall and handsome, with a proud carriage and winsome smile, a successful career and high hopes for a good life for his young wife and children. And I pictured him with my mother beside him, as I have seen them in old photographs, she petite and slender, her 5'4" frame standing happily against his 6'2", her deep-set eyes looking thoughtfully into the future with the man who adored her, who fought for her against his family's objections, and who waited four long years to call her his wife. The father before me still retained traces of someone who loves life to the fullest and for whom family ties, whether as son, husband, or father, were sacred responsibilities.

Then we talked of the future, of what it might be like to go to another country, to start life anew in a foreign land where we knew neither the language nor the customs, and of the difficulties of being immigrants rather than natives.

"America is a land of immigrants," we all agreed, and fantasized of going to the land of "golden opportunities." To the exaggerated, immensely romanticized version of America with which we filled our daydreams both at home and at school, I added my own flights of fancy, which I embellished with the best from every fairy tale or story I ever read, and transferred it to the mythical land three thousand miles across the ocean. I gave it all the attributes that were missing in our present circumstances and transformed it into a land where there exists no hunger, no hard labor, no hate for people of another race, faith, or origin. America was Cinderella dancing with her prince, who had rescued her from a life of poverty and servitude. It was the Promised Land and President Roosevelt our Moses.

Thus we dreamed to make the present more tolerable and the future less threatening.

Another reality stepped into our lives in 1940 with air raids by the RAF, the Royal Air Force. The passing of each day and each night felt like a lifetime. The young grew old quickly and wise beyond their years. Though we did not see the whole truth with the eyes of adults, what we did know was chiseled into our consciousness like ancient runes into stones, the meaning of it only partly decipherable.

Awareness of the reality awaiting us was a fearful thing, a thing of death. And we wanted life.

One day in 1940, I told my mother, who was preparing our noon meal and was not really listening to me, that a girl had come to school crying. My words got lost amidst the clatter of pots and pans until I mentioned the word *Umsiedlung*, relocation. My mother stopped what she was doing and looked at me with eyes full of fear. Once I knew that I had her attention, I told her from beginning to end what I had heard.

"Eva told us that her mother's brother, who lives in Stettin with his wife and three small children, had all been deported to Lublin, somewhere in Poland. Eva's parents received a postcard from them with only a very brief note on it, the rest had all been crossed out with black ink. What was left to read was a request for food and warm clothes, especially blankets for the children. Do we have anything to give away?"

My mother looked at me and then averted her eyes. She did not respond right away, perhaps thinking more about the news than an answer to my question. "I'll try," she promised, with her back turned away to hide her feelings.

From that day on, it became common practice to have "drives" of collecting food or clothes as we learned of more and more people being "relocated." The packages contained canned goods, legumes, soap, toothpaste and whatever warm clothes anyone could spare. My aunts in Biesdorf found an old blanket in their attic and my mother's sister contributed some toilet articles from her store.

The postcards coming from these *Arbeitslager*, labor camps, as they were called on the deportation notices, were heavily censored and thus reduced to brief messages requesting either food, toilet articles or whatever else was needed. They all ended with a statement that the deportees were well and working.

Then came the notifications telling family members that the internee had died. The cause given for their unexpected death was always a natural one, either heart failure or pneumonia. The notice was accompanied by a small container holding the ashes of the deceased.

We listened to these accounts with profound skepticism, though the word "murdered" was never uttered.

We tried to imagine what it must be like in one of those *Arbeitslag*, what kind of work people were ordered to do, what kind of food they were given.

We talked of people dying, not being killed, for we were lacking the evidence and the imagination as well to picture the manner of their deaths.

We wanted to believe the official explanation of "natural" causes, but were haunted by one question - natural under what conditions?

We recalled the stories told by those who had returned from Sachsenhausen or Dachau after their arrest during the pogrom of November 9-10, 1938, and we asked ourselves, what human being can for long endure hunger and cold, hard labor and little rest, beatings and malnutrition, disease without proper medical attention, without succumbing to the body's limitations to withstand such abuse?

We were asking questions repeatedly: who will be next? Who will soon share their fate? And finally: how would we meet that fate?

With the rising tensions and uncertainties in the Jewish community, my friendship with Mira was beginning to change.

"It is not good to rely so much on one friendship alone." My father and I were once again engaged in an argument about my friendship with Mira, which he viewed with grave reservations. Over long periods of time he could remain a silent observer, but on occasions when what he saw troubled him, he became a vociferous critic of what he considered an unbalanced relationship.

"You need to make other friends," was his usual defense for finding fault with the dynamic that governed how Mira and I related to each other. "You mustn't allow Mira to be so possessive, to claim so much of your energy and attention."

"I do have other friends," was my usual, rather defensive, response. "There is Rita Orbach, who is also Mira's friend, there is Renate Pless, Eva Jakubek, and Vera, whom you have seen here a few times. Mira just happens to be my best friend and I am hers. She gets upset when she feels slighted for someone else, and I don't want to upset her. It brings on seizures."

"There you are," my father latched onto that point. "That's exactly what I mean. She may use her illness to demand your exclusive attention and that's not fair to you. Her jealousy is preventing you from getting closer to other friends."

The argument would continue, with my defense of Mira against my father's urgent warnings. Nonetheless, he had stirred up feelings in me that I could not ignore. There were indeed some troubling aspects to our relationship that disturbed me as well, but I would never admit to my father that his observations and conclusions carried some measure of truth, fearing that he might insist I terminate my friendship with Mira altogether, something I could not ever see myself doing. On days when I especially felt the oppressive element in Mira's irrational jealousies and demands for my undivided attention to her alone, I turned to my mother for advice and understanding. She gave me suggestions of how to handle Mira's temper tantrums over my alleged neglect of her.

"All that Mira needs to hear from you is that your friendship matters a great deal to you, that you are not going to replace your closeness to her with anyone else. You can definitely convince her of that, I am sure."

My mother's counsel sounded reasonable, but when I tried to put it into practice, Mira accepted my assurances with obvious reluctance. A small frown, knitted across her eyebrows, told me clearly that she did not quite believe me. And I could not always be sure whether I believed them wholeheartedly, whether I was feeling sorry for her or, as my father had correctly divined it, I made unnecessary concessions to her illness. Her need for my undivided loyalty, my total commitment to her alone at the expense of having other close friends, except for those we shared together, struck me as being so much more than ordinary jealousy, so absolute and unrealistic, that I made no attempt to meet her demands. To counter her irrationality with reason seemed futile to me, with the result that I accused myself of dishonesty in being with her. What I wanted to protect in our friendship was a genuine and deep kinship, which her inner turmoil held in abeyance.

There was one issue, however, about which I could not feel quite as sanguine as I did about her jealousy, giving rise to serious doubts whether I had a true friend in her. That issue concerned my Jewishness. Because of my mother's "Aryan" status, in Nazi terminology, she considered me less Jewish than herself and thought of me as being somehow immune to Nazi persecution, despite all the facts to the contrary, and despite my mother's conversion to Judaism. Whenever Mira raised the subject of my being a *Mischling* (of mixed blood), a term I despised and which Mira always pronounced with a ring of disdain in her voice, I felt rage and pain at her facile adoption of labels applied by the Nuremberg Laws of racial discrimination. I was raised to think of myself as fully Jewish and clung to that tenaciously. To hear Mira question this was an affront I did not expect from a friend. Memories of my baptism, the sense of betrayal I had felt, the guilt of having gone through with it, all contributed to my feeling vulnerable and defensive when faced with Mira's taunts. At times I thought my secret must be so transparent that Mira could read it off my forehead.

"You can't really know what it is like to be a *Volljude*," Mira would usually start these quarrels.

"I do know," I replied, my voice rising with anger already at her easy assumption. "I feel it... inside... I experience being Jewish just as much as you do. I practice it... Why do you want to play Hitler's racist game and divide us?"

Resentment grew big in me at the very thought of being excluded, being set apart by one of my own, of having to justify myself on a matter that needed no justification, only acceptance.

"Hitler hasn't made any distinctions between us so far, has he?" I tried to make her see the truth of that at least.

"He will," she answered with such confidence as if she had been privy to arcane Gestapo documents. "The Nuremberg Laws will protect you, you'll see," she claimed vindictively.

Her last remark, with its callousness, shocked me into silence and helpless frustration. I had to suppress the urge to slap her right there, in the middle of a busy Berlin street. How could a friend say this? My thoughts came out as an accusation as I turned to face her.

"You are no friend," I lashed out with hot conviction.

I walked away without another word.

That was our last fray about my Jewishness. She had been so upset, she told me later, that she had had an attack that same evening, albeit a mild one. She also had a change of heart, no doubt the result of having talked to her parents about the incident. She apologized to me and admitted, echoing her parent's words, that it was folly to fight about one's beliefs, and that she would try never to start a fight again.

If there was one discernible and predictable pattern to Mira's epileptic seizures, they mirrored her state of mind. Any incident that caused her emotional distress, such as our fights, or that presented a threat to her safety, such as Gestapo activities and the bombing of Berlin, was followed by a seizure within hours, depending on the severity of the incident. The spectre of death, whether from bombs or from the Gestapo, stalked all our lives, but whereas the strain of having to live in a constant state of terror takes inward forms, leaving less immediate, visible marks on most of us, it showed starkly in Mira's convulsed body whenever a new threat arose which, with air raids increasing, was fairly often. Her need for our friendship then I accepted willingly.

The flames of hatred towards Jews increased with slogans and incendiary speeches by Hitler and Goebbels against the British and the Jews. Many believed them; the terror so close to their doorstep prompted many to look for a culprit for all their losses. The Jew, as the "other," lesser known neighbor, was an easy target.

Mira and I discussed these speeches, meant to instill hatred in people against those we loved, and we often wondered how effective the venom of their rhetoric was. Once Mira realized that I was not exempt from the perils that faced *Volljuden*, our friendship shifted onto more common ground; we took refuge in what united rather than what divided us. There were, after all, so many occasions for talk, for laughter, for tears, for sharing secrets, and so much need for holding on to something stable when the earth was literally shaking underneath us. The tremors of a human catastrophe were constant reminders of life's fragility. Our quarrels started to look minuscule against a spectre of much larger proportion.

There were rumors that the air raids were being carried out by the Royal Air Force in retaliation for the bombing of London which official sources in Berlin denied, claiming the bombing of London had been an accident. Hitler, livid with rage about the attacks on German civilians, vowed vengeance: ruthless, calculated vengeance. We knew we were in for a long period of death and destruction from the skies. The newspapers had called the British pilots *Luftpiraten, Terroristen*. Of course, German pilots bombing civilians in London was not terrorism but warfare, an act of defense. *Die Welt steht auf dem Kopf* (the world is standing on its head), my father used to comment, and our co-tenant, Frau Schmidt, shook her head and added her favorite word, *Wahnsinn* (madness).

People at first talked non-stop about these bombings: where they occurred, the damage done to buildings and human lives, and the rescue efforts by other citizens. My father made feeble attempts to allay our fear of these nightly visitors from the sky with a humorous remark. "At least the bombs don't know who is a Jew and who is an Aryan - they haven't read the Nuremberg Laws." It was poor consolation.

The blackouts every night also made no distinction between Jew and non-Jew and cloaked everyone in anonymity. The strict adherence to keep the city in darkness was so effective that people collided with each other on the streets until someone had the ingenious idea to introduce phosphorous buttons that glowed in the dark. Suddenly the streets were full of little will-o'-the-wisps to lighten our paths and remove some of the gloom.

We had to live through another celebration of Hitler's birthday. No one could escape its tumultuous observance. Loudspeakers blasted out nationalistic songs, military parades with banners flying high and drums pounding out the beat for the marchers inundated the streets, while throngs of cheering citizens choked up the sidewalks.

All that had taken place on a Sunday, but it had certainly not been a day of rest. For those of us who recoiled in horror at this vulgar display of power, the day had all the markings of our own funeral. I had listened to a speech by Hitler on Frau Schmidt's radio and the message sickened my soul. How could anyone harbor so much hatred?

———

The day after the celebration of Hitler's birthday on April 20, 1941, Mira waited for me as usual at the corner of her street, Krummestrasse, from where we would walk to school together. I could tell from the expression on her face that she was preoccupied, but I deliberately avoided asking her why she looked so upset; the need to rid myself of what I had heard the day before took precedence over Mira's mood. I started telling Mira what was foremost in my mind. She listened for a while, then interrupted me in the middle of a sentence to ask why I had subjected myself to such *Unrat*, such garbage. I quoted what Frau Schmidt had told us when she invited us to listen to Hitler on her radio, "Know your enemy, so you can be on your guard."

"You should have heard him," I continued, ignoring Mira's lack of interest. "It was chilling. The man screamed himself hoarse - on his birthday, mind you - and you could hear him bang his fist on the lectern to emphasize every hideous word he hurled at his audience. The words came out of him like molten lava. It scorched my insides."

All through his speech, I had difficulty recognizing the same language in which I said my prayers, recited poetry aloud to myself, and in which our family communicated our loves and our resentments. The most frightful irony of his speech was the impression he wanted to create of being the victim rather than the victimizer of the alleged Jewish-Bolshevik conspiracy, and of the enemies of the Third Reich, the British pilots. "But we will prevail," he had bellowed in a spasm of triumph that nearly broke his voice. The audience had cheered and shouted, *"Heil Hitler! Sieg Heil!"* over and over again. All of us sitting around the radio had looked at each other in disbelief. My throat felt tight like a drum, holding in the words. Frau Schmidt, breaking the pall of silence, managed to say, *"Der Mann ist wahnsinnig,* (the man is a lunatic). He should be locked up or we'll all end up in an *Irrenanstalt,* an insane asylum."

The image she conjured up corresponded so well to my own impressions that I nodded my head and was glad to hear in her voice such loathing and anguish for the evil that spilled over from the man and ignited evil in others. Although Hitler's raving rhetoric wrenched my guts, speeches by Goebbels incited an even greater terror in me, because his voice never rose above the volume appropriate to a public speaker, and the hatred in it was of a more cerebral, better-articulated nature. Goebbels' speeches by comparison seemed rational rather than visceral like Hitler's. Goebbels had the intelligence and the verbal power to manipulate the minds of his listeners into believing what he wanted them to believe. There was more danger in appealing to their reason than to their passions. Reason is like flint compared to passion's flame.

"At the end of Hitler's speech I felt cut off from my own future," I confessed to Mira.

After letting me talk to the end, Mira finally said, "We can all expect to receive Hitler's birthday present for Jews."

"What do you mean?" I asked, troubled by her doomsday voice.

"Well, that's what my father told us after he had received his lay-off notice together with a draft for *Zwangsarbeit*," Mira explained.

"*Zwangsarbeit*...? What is that supposed to mean?"

"It's a new ordinance. Forced labor for Jews. Apparently they need workers for the war industry now that so many factory workers have been called to the front to fight for... well... you know. They are replacing the workers with Jews taken from their jobs and my father is among them. He has been assigned to *Siemens Werke*, starting in two days."

Some time elapsed before this news settled in my consciousness. I thought of Hitler's speech and could not believe how quickly word and action could follow each other. I heard Mira's voice as though coming from some distance, "Your father is sure to be called too."

Mira's prediction came true all too soon.

I was coming home from school one afternoon and saw my father back from work earlier than usual, sitting in his chair, looking dejected. His expression - the corners of his mouth always turned down when he was heavy with thought - told me what I knew already. He gave us the news in a muffled voice. Since there was no more emigration for Jews, his job at the *Jüdische Gemeinde* was finished and he had been drafted to forced labor. The notice had been handed to him the moment he entered his office.

"I have to report for work at Anhalter Bahnhof. Working hours are from 7 a.m. to 6 p.m. Hope I'll make it through the day."

As in 1933, my father was again among the first to lose his job because of another law to remove Jews from regular positions.

Once my father started his forced labor, life at home resembled a ship whose ballast was out of balance. All our attention and care shifted to him. We worried about him when he came home, and we worried about him when he was at work. The strain of doing hard physical labor for eleven hours a day for a man of forty-three who had worked in offices most of his life showed to an alarming degree. He was near collapse in the evenings, afraid to face another day and wondering whether he would get through it. He was losing weight rapidly and, what took an even greater toll on him, his outlook was close to despair. The thought of days stretching into weeks, weeks into months and years of unremitting hardship until his body could no longer obey the commands forced upon it by the state, weighed on him even more crushingly than the heavy loads from the freight trains he had to lift for eleven hours a day. He was not as afraid of dying of "natural" causes, like exhaustion, as he was of being shipped off to a camp in Poland, away from his family, away from hope, if his strength should fail him entirely.

He envied the stamina of his German co-workers who had been doing this work for years and whose physical strength was bolstered by a proper amount of food, something denied to Jews. Perhaps, my father speculated, it might be easier on him if he could work on a full stomach.

Our ration cards, all stamped with a "J", had been greatly curtailed in comparison to those of other citizens. *Nicht genug zum Leben, und zu viel zum Sterben* ("not enough for living and too much for dying") was the general saying among us who received no meat, fish, dairy products, fruit, vegetables, white bread, and no coupons for textiles or tobacco. Lack of sleep because of air raids that lasted two to three hours in the middle of the night caused fatigue and lethargy for nearly everyone. This, along with malnutrition, sapped whatever energies my father may have had in reserve. Despite the terror and noise during an air raid, my father often caught up on much needed sleep sitting in our shelter in the cellar.

After weeks of this ordeal, he came home one day with an unexpected surprise. We could see the change in him the minute he entered the door. His face was bright with an impish smile; a rather furtive look in his eyes prepared us for some very private revelation. Straightening his shoulders to his full six feet two, he fished something out of his pocket and put it on the dining room table. "Cheese," he said simply, beaming with satisfaction. "*Butterkäse* from Norway."

We stared at him, the questions caught in our throats, but then he volunteered the answer. "Everybody is doing it," he reassured us, seeing our worried faces while he looked more and more like a schoolboy who has cheated on an exam and gotten away with it. Everyone unloading the freight cars, he explained, has started to steal some of its goods to take home to their families because even for them the rations were insufficient.

"And they let you... a Jew... in on the act?" my mother asked, still doubtful, since stealing goods belonging to the state was considered sabotage, and it was no secret what happened to saboteurs. My father again assured us that every one of his German co-workers knew that Jews were in greater need of food and besides, they had started to worry about his deteriorating condition and were aware of the consequences if one day he could no longer serve the Reich by working.

"They want to help. They are simple, decent, working class people, *anständige Kerle*." My father defended them with such ardor that it greatly diminished our fears, at least for that day.

During supper, we were eager to listen to his Robin Hood adventures, the return of his former sense of humor. My mother divided the piece of cheese, the size of a large bar of soap, evenly between the four of us. "Try to make it last for more than one meal," she suggested, but we paid her no heed, too anxious to spread this golden gift over our ration of black bread. "The bread has never tasted so good," Hans commented and, with our mouths full, we nodded in happy agreement. This is what manna must have tasted like to the ancient Israelites stranded in the desert after years of deprivation and loss of hope. We had almost forgotten the taste of cheese.

From that day on, my father brought home the same *Butterkäse* whenever it was safe to do so. As he gained more expertise and confidence in these contraband operations, the sizes of the blocks of cheese increased in proportion. At first we used it sparingly, trying to make it last until the next, unpredictable trainload full of this ambrosia arrived. As my father became more daring and we the hungrier for it, the amount of cheese on our black bread swelled into big hunks until we came close to developing an aversion to it and asked whether he couldn't manage some variety of flavor the next time. But *Butterkäse* was all the conquering troops could add to their war booty.

My mother had the perfect idea of sewing extra pockets inside my father's coat for the express purpose of carrying home ever larger quantities of this precious source of life. The thought that these stolen goods were spoils of war taken from conquered lands crossed our minds for as long as it takes to wipe away a tear.

The change in my father was nothing short of a miracle. He attacked his daily chores like a man with a mission, a purpose, a challenge. He was our warrior. He was our David fighting Goliath. Keeping starvation from his family consumed his waking hours and gave him hope. It seemed to lighten the burden of his physical hardships and was noticeable even in his gait. He walked with a firmer step as if to arm himself for the next new and dangerous foray. He loved to give us witty accounts of his "cheesy" adventures. He had discovered a new side of himself and relished it.

Some time in the evening before the first of September, 1941, my mother is sewing the yellow star on all our outer garments. I am watching her - stitch by stitch - my eyes riveted on the object of our disgrace - the bilious yellow, the black lines framing the Star of David, the word *Jude* written in imitation Hebrew letters right in the center. The image burns itself into my heart and fills me with dread when I think of having to wear it in public the next day.

"I hate them... I hate them..." the words tumble out of my mouth as if another had spoken them, as if they had taken on a life of their own, freed from the long prison of silence. I recognize them as something that has always been true, though concealed like a snake under a rock.

My mother looks at me, not in reprimand, but with infinite pain and sadness in her deep eyes, eyes that speak to me of her helplessness and anguish, since she does not have to share the experience of having to wear the star.

"I understand, Rita, I truly do," she says quietly with a deep sigh. "But there are too many to hate, too many for your young heart to contain. Don't poison your heart with hatred, that is what they want, that would give them the final victory. Hate Evil, not the evildoers," she concludes, her voice trailing off into her own thoughts.

I cannot understand how she can be so calm. What is Evil, anyway? It doesn't have a face, a shape, a voice, whereas people do. How can I hate the faceless, shapeless, voiceless existence of something that is beyond sight and sound? Whatever Evil is, it works through people. Evil is something I can see and hear, such as what comes from the men in black and grey uniforms, marching through the streets, singing the praises of the man we abhor. Or the speeches of Hitler and Goebbels. I can hear Evil pouring out of their mouths. They are the conduits of Evil, I can hate them and their mind-wrenching denunciations of the people I love. If Evil speaks through them, then I will hate Evil.

My father is preparing us for tomorrow when we must appear in public with our yellow stars fastened on our coats. He is struggling for words, and a tense silence hangs in the room before he begins to speak.

"Tomorrow will be a difficult day for all of us, we know that, and words are hardly enough to prepare you for it. It is hard to predict how people will react to seeing us marked with this yellow mockery. The first reaction will be one of shock, I'm sure, but beyond that... who knows? Some may taunt us...we have to expect that. Others may look away in silent embarrassment. Each will have an unpredictable response to it. I guess what I am trying to tell you is... I mean, we can't worry too much about their response, we can only think of what we need to do. Here I can only counsel you to remain calm, strong, and walk with your head erect, and sort of... sort of build a wall around yourself, an invisible wall of innocence. I know this will be difficult, but remember... we have done nothing wrong to be thus stigmatized."

We then speak of this new measure as another test, another call to maintain our dignity in the face of degradation, our faith in our innocence despite the slander, our love of our tradition in the face of hate, our undeserved fate living under a regime that acts in defiance of respect for God's children.

We speak of the real significance of the Star of David in Jewish history and my father reminds us, as he did before with the names of "Israel" and "Sara," that the Magen David, though satirized and debased now in the cloth badge before us, is the sacred symbol of Judaism, as is the cross for Christians. Jewish warriors have fought under it in defense of their faith; Jews have prayed under it in times of peril and of peace in synagogues all over the world.

"Use it like a shield tomorrow, to arm yourself against any possible hurt that may come to you from a hostile stranger," my father counsels before he sits back in his chair, giving in to his own troubled thoughts.

"Just remember that there is nothing wrong with who you are," my mother reiterates, "and let that knowledge - and God - guide your steps tomorrow."

It sounds so reasonable within the safe confines of our living room, our shelter, but will it suffice tomorrow? Hans and I will have to walk to school alone since my father leaves much earlier for work at Schlesischer Bahnhof.

The next day proceeds contrary to our worst expectations. When Hans and I come face to face with the first pedestrians, my resolve of last night to stay strong fails me and I feel as though my legs are no longer a part of me. But then I notice, to my relief, that hardly anyone is looking at us directly, no one is staring at us or smiling in derision. Some avoid looking at us altogether, their eyes averted deliberately, it seems, while others have a vaguely pained or embarrassed expression on their faces. A few smile at us furtively, their eyes conveying impotent sympathy.

Suddenly there are other yellow stars appearing on people who, like us, do not fit the much advertised stereotype of a Jew as depicted in Nazi propaganda newspapers and posters. We exchange knowing glances of recognition. Gone is the sense of isolation, gone the fear as we pass more and more people wearing the star. I never knew there were so many Jews living in our neighborhood. Now an invisible hand weaves together the separate strands of our fortunes into a strong pattern of unity.

Thank God, we are not alone.

The exposure of our Jewish identity to the public at large made our vulnerability from then on an inescapable reality. No longer able to hide behind our "Nordic" looks, as is true for many Jews in Germany, we could no longer hide our fears as well, whether in public or at home.

Out on the streets, our eyes no longer cast around to look at passing scenes, but were looking straight ahead or on the ground as though we could thus shut out possible dangers coming from passersby.

At home, past fears of becoming a ready catch for ardent Nazis, as in my father's earlier warnings not to attract the attention of the men in the brown uniforms, was turning from a distant probability into a daily and very real possibility. We had to attach the Star of David next to our father's name plate outside our apartment, like an invitation to any who wanted to catch Jews. Frau Schmidt, to whom we confided our fear of easy capture, had tried to have the star removed from our front door, under the pretext that she, as an "Aryan," objected to this defilement. The answer she received was simple. She could move to another apartment occupied only by "Aryans." She declined the offer and the star remained next to our name on the front door.

The fear of easy capture created tensions between my father and myself, which I interpreted at the time as expressions of his ownership of my personhood rather than what it was: fear of losing his children to the Nazi beast on the prowl for Jewish blood.

That fear was most manifest when I came home from school later than expected, even if it was just a matter of ten or fifteen minutes. It gave rise to arguments between us where nothing I would say in my defense could assuage his near panic. Talking to a friend after school, making a detour to see a friend home, was not accepted as an excuse nor did it relieve his agitation. I was the cruel and inconsiderate daughter who did not respect her father's justified concerns.

My mother would then have to be the mediator between father and daughter and lessen the bitterness that threatened to divide us. She would sympathize with both of us and try to make me understand his overriding anxiety, but every time my father and I had another spat, I was the oppressed child again and my father the oppressor. I simply could not or would not understand how he could begrudge me the only pleasure available to me - to spend time with friends as any normal child would. His objections to it made me feel like a delinquent with abnormal desires. That we were living in abnormal times was not something I was yet ready to absorb, despite all the obvious signs. I wanted to ignore the signs, and friendships offered me that escape into a world free of nagging adults.

Ever since we were made to wear the yellow star, the issue of my Jewishness for Mira was laid to rest once and for all. More than ever, she was the one person I could confide in.

So it was that one day, while we were walking to school, I had to unburden myself of the sadness left in me after my mother brought home the news the evening before. It was a day in October, an autumn day, permeated with all the signs of another cold winter on the way. The weather, cold and wet, the gray sky, suited my mood and loosened my tongue.

"My mother came home last night with bad news about my grandmother, who has taken to her bed entirely," I began telling Mira.

Mira, remembering the death of her own grandmother a few years ago, turned her attention to me, waiting for me to tell her more about my "Oma."

In all the years I could remember, I had never seen my grandmother move out of the chair at the kitchen table against the wall near the door. From that spot, she exerted as strong a presence in my life as any of the more active members of the family. My image of my grandmother is confined to that one corner in the kitchen where she spent her days watching life go on around her as a passive observer, dependent on people to do things for her.

Whenever we would come for visits, our expectation to find her in that chair in the kitchen was never disappointed. There she sat, hands folded in her lap, her feet resting on a low footstool and, on cold days, a blanket that reached the floor spread over her knees. She smiled at us in greeting, a tense and strained smile in a closed and serious face. Her lips were usually tightly compressed as if to keep in words or stifle a cry of pain. I seldom heard her laugh out loud, and in all our social gatherings she was more like an outsider than a participant. She always listened to our reports of the day's events but seldom gave her comments or advice. Her world had shrunk to that one corner from which she could hear her grandchildren play and listen to their chatter near or far. On rare occasions, my grandfather or her daughters would move her chair into the front room to celebrate birthdays or holidays. It was always a painful process for her to be moved and she would wince in pain.

Her difficulties started with varicose veins, the result of standing on a cold cement floor for years while working behind the counter of her store. Her condition worsened when she developed open sores which, always alive in my memory, would not heal and had to be tended to every day by a change of dressings. Her two daughters, Tante Liesel and my mother, were saddled with this task. I always associated my grandmother with pain. My mother and aunt shielded us from witnessing the worst moments of her agony and never changed her dressings in our presence. I was there a few times by accident and saw her open wounds and watched her face; my mind let down its shutters to keep out empathy.

"Now the kitchen might forever be empty of her presence," I said to Mira, trying to visualize the vacant corner in the kitchen. "I remember what she said to me after our synagogue was burned down: 'Now you must carry your synagogue in your heart,' and she wasn't even Jewish. But she understood. The first time she saw the yellow star on us she shook her head and sighed, '*Was für'n Bloedsinn*,' (what craziness) and wiped away a tear. Politics for her was a kind of madness, and she wanted to hear none of it. I'll miss her if she dies."

A few days after this conversation, my mother entered our apartment after a visit with her mother and asked us to sit down. What she had to tell us came as expected.

"Oma died early this morning. I would like you to come and look at her. She is lying in the front room." Her voice was steady and calm.

The idea of seeing a dead person filled me with repugnance and my first response was to blurt out "No, I won't..." but seeing the pained look in my mother's eyes stopped me, aware that I had hurt her in her grief. She took my hand in hers and spoke to me in words distinct and deliberate, as if she had rehearsed them in expectation of my refusal.

"Rita, there is nothing to be afraid of. You are now thirteen years old and the idea of death is surely no stranger to you. Oma died in her sleep... peacefully and free from pain. And that is how she looks now... peaceful. I would not ask you to come and see her if I thought you were not strong and brave enough to say good-bye to your Oma. She would like it and I know you might learn something about her you never knew."

My curiosity was aroused. My mother's calm composure and confident manner at a time like this impressed me immensely and instilled trust in me so that I felt compelled to relinquish my initial reluctance and follow her wishes. I insisted, nevertheless, that she stay with me throughout the moments when I would look upon death for the first time. She promised to do so, but as we approached my grandmother's store, I wanted to change my mind and turn back. At other times I had been glad to have the store so near to our home, but on that day I wished it were in another city so that I could have more time to strengthen my resolve.

"*Komm, Püppchen,*" my mother urged gently, "and say your final farewell to Oma. You'll be glad you did, trust me."

My mother went ahead of me and I followed hesitantly, still not at all sure if I wanted to go through with it. She opened the door to the front room, a place associated in my mind with only happy times, and motioned me to enter the room that had become my grandmother's resting place. While I had been walking slowly behind my mother, I had followed the expression on her face. The tranquil look and the inviting smile emboldened me to go nearer the bed on which my grandmother lay. It was alongside the same wall as the door.

"You see... she looks happy now..." my mother said, and for the first time I could detect a slight tremor in her voice, a kind of mournful joy. At her last remark, I finally turned my head to look at my dead grandmother. I felt no horror, only amazement. I also marveled at my aunt's willingness to give up her bed to a dead woman, the same bed she had slept in for years and would do so again after my grandmother had been laid to her final rest.

My grandmother looked as though she were asleep. I had trouble seeing in her the woman I had known all my life. She looked ever so much smaller, frailer. And her face, usually etched with pain, looked smooth and serene. I thought I saw a faint smile tucked into the corners of her mouth, erasing all my former conceptions of death as some sort of gargoyle. My mother had been right, she looked at peace, her hands folded over her chest, the same hands I remembered lying folded in her lap while alive. She appeared to be in a deep and restful sleep, a healing sleep from which she would awaken cured and whole again. The smile at the corners of her mouth seemed to want to tell me something, a secret I would never know and that she took to her grave, a legacy for us to try and unravel. I received this smile as a gift, her last gift by which she wanted to be remembered, casting a gentler light over all the memories of her painful life on earth.

I wanted to remember her the way she looked then, at peace and freed from pain, rather than the way she was when alive, weighed down by years of an unwanted life.

We each said good-bye to her in our own way without speaking. My mother repeated what she had said earlier.

"You see how tranquil she looks. That was the way she always looked before her illness. That is the reason I wanted you to come. She is telling us to rejoice with her for being liberated from her long suffering. Death has set her free, something she always wanted, welcoming death as a friend. There is sadness for her leaving us, but joy for the end to her suffering."

My mother and I left the room together, neither one of us crying. There was a calmness that enfolded us both and guided our steps back to the world of the living. I was grateful to Oma for giving us that calm.

A new wave of intimidations and finite actions engulfed the Jewish community a few months after the introduction of the yellow star. Having met with no outcry from its non-Jewish citizenry against this mockery of Judaism's sacred symbol, it was as though the government had been given permission to set in motion its death machine for the Final Solution of the Jewish problem. It was not that all Germans gave their consent to it, but a passive acceptance of the status quo, however repugnant it may have been for many, fostered the fear of open resistance.

Reports were soon circulating that Jews were summoned to appear at designated places throughout the city with a prescribed amount of their belongings - as much as they could carry in two hands. The rest of their property and money was confiscated by the state. We heard from friends that they were allowed to take only bare essentials with them on their journey to unknown destinations. We learned some of the details from my friend, Rita Orbach, whose grandparents had received their notice one day and were gone the next; there had hardly been time for a farewell. Such sudden departures were occurring more and more frequently, particularly of the elderly, leaving their families with two questions: where are they taking them and will we see them again?

Another girl from my class, Mia Mendelsohn, reported to us that the elderly couple next door to them had committed joint suicide to avoid deportation. They had preferred a voluntary death to a forced one. Cases of suicides were reported all over the city.

The deportations proceeded at first in quite an orderly way and with some warnings. The people targeted had some time to choose what to take and to say farewell to their immediate family members. They received notice to be ready in a day or two.

And finally it happened. The inevitable fate planned for Jews in Germany entered our family without warning. The Gestapo had gone to the home of my father's Onkel Hugo and Tante Helene, an elderly couple, and had taken them away. My father gave us this news in a broken voice, benumbed by sadness. He told us how he had learned of their arrest. A former colleague from his days at Jüdische Gemeinde had met him on the train riding home. Visibly upset, he told my father that he was now working at the collection center in Grosse Hamburgerstrasse where those to be shipped off with the next transport were held. It was there that he had been asked by our uncle and aunt to take their last message to the outside world. "Tell our nephew, Fritz Kuhn, where we are."

"They will have to go," my father sighed, "these wonderful people, and we will never know where. It's terrible to think of them having to face unimaginable hardships."

We sat around the dining room table and remembered them. Onkel Hugo was so proud and strong-willed, with few resources to withstand the new harsh conditions, even if he had been younger. And Tante Helene... of delicate stature and frail health... how could she possibly adjust to work camp life or to whatever other place they would be sent? Those dear people. We could not imagine them anywhere but in their modest apartment on Grollmannstrasse. What was to become of them?

We exchanged our memories of these people, who had brought so much grace and warmth into our lives and we felt closer to them than ever. They had always welcomed us into their home with the smell of freshly baked *Kuchen* greeting us as soon as we entered their apartment, furnished with subdued elegance and dotted with souvenirs from Tante Helene's many trips around Europe. The windows were covered with lace curtains from France and Belgium where she traveled countless times to buy lace for the department store where she worked for many years. My mother especially reminded us of the quiet dignity of Tante Helene, the affection with which, from the start of my parents' courtship, she alone of my father's family had accepted my mother without hesitation. Everyone else had clung to their objections to an alliance between a Jew and a Gentile, a prosperous businessman and a working-class girl.

"But Tante Helene was different," my mother recalled. "She was a woman of the world, had met many kinds of people in her travels and had learned to accept them in all their diversities of creed and social status."

We mourned for them as if they were dead already.

We were in the midst of 1942. Word was out that all Jewish schools would have to close as of July first. Hardly anything shocked us anymore, though the ordinance in March of that same year, forbidding Jews the use of public transportation, except from home to work and back again with a special permit, sent tremors through the Jewish community, since it meant we were going to be cut off from family and friends who did not live within walking distance. We knew what would happen if we violated this new law; besides, with the yellow star in full view, the possibilities of transgressions were greatly diminished as we thought of patrols asking for our travel permits. To remove the star was, we knew, suicidal.

The closing of Jewish schools sent a clear message to the Jewish youth: they were to have no future except that planned for them by the state. My class was fortunate in that the closing coincided with our graduation day. Hans's education was truncated two years before he was to graduate.

Not long after my class had celebrated its graduation, we received our draft notices for forced labor. I was fourteen years old. Mira and I looked at our notices with the place of work assigned to each of us. We stared at each other in disbelief. We had been assigned to the same munitions factory somewhere in Steglitz; the date to start work was set for July sixth, a Monday. That gave us two weeks to bid farewell to our childhood.

"Do you think...?" Mira finally asked me and I, anticipating the rest of her question, shook my head in definite denial and answered her. "No, no... never. They would never deliberately have assigned us to the same work place because they know we are friends or... because they know of your seizures. No... that would be too kind."

Mira Holzheim, my unforgettable friend

My father Fritz Kuhn

My mother Frieda Kuhn

My father (baby Fritz Kuhn) and
his grandfather Herz Kuhn

Engagement of Fritz and
Frieda Kuhn, 1922

Frieda in Switzerland

Frieda having fun!

The Kuhn family with my
brother Hans and me

My brother Hans "embarrassed"

Me playing with my doll and pushcart

My cousin Klaus and me

My first day at school
holding a cornucopia

My brother Hans and me

Synagogue in Fasanenstrasse before the night of broken glass

I am with Klaus and Hans, visiting our aunts' home in the country with an abundance of cherry trees before the war, 1939

Forced laborers who
worked with me

Felizitas, daughter of
a Gestapo agent

My post-war friend
Ruth Silverberg

A great photo of
my brother Hans

The Kuhn family after the war, 1947

Here I am in Boston after the war having fun!

My children in front of my home in Berkeley, CA
Ruth, Kenneth, Sarah, and Rachel

My grandchildren Benjamin, Ilse, Ariana, Ilya, and Irit

Chapter 4

In the Eye of the Hurricane

Turning and turning in the widening gyre,
The falcon cannot hear the falconer.
Things fall apart, the center cannot hold,
Mere anarchy is loosed upon the world.
The blood-dimmed tide is loosed, and everywhere
the ceremony of innocence is drowned.
The best lack all conviction, while the worst
are full of passionate intensity.
—WILLIAM BUTLER YEATS, *"The Second Coming"*

The fires of November 9, 1938 had long since died down, leaving the charred ruins of synagogues and broken human lives as constant reminders that the sparks of hatred still burned and could be ignited to a greater conflagration. By 1942, Jews in Berlin were left with no doubt that other, less visible flames had taken the place of those earlier ones and were burning as well in the hearts of those planning the *Umsiedlung*, the relocation of Jews to camps in the East. Unfamiliar names like Litzmannstadt, Minsk, Riga, were mentioned frequently in connection with people who were forced to resettle in one of them, under the pretext that they were needed for *Arbeit fürs Reich*, work for the Reich, of which they were no longer citizens. The cynical contradiction in that escaped no one. We, the potential targets of this program, knew it to be a euphemism for the planned removal of a disposable minority of the German population: its Jewish citizens.

The cries for "*Juden Raus*," heard and read so many times, were becoming an actuality.

Those deported were at first allowed to send mail to family members, usually in the form of pre-printed postcards. They regularly and without fail contained requests for food and warm clothes, ending with reassurances that all was well, that they were working. We asked ourselves how could all be well with them if they were in constant need of food and clothes? And what might happen to them if they were no longer capable of working? What about the old, the sick, and the very young children who were surely not fit to work for the armament of the Reich? Those left behind in Berlin who had been drafted to forced labor, like my father, were haunted by the fear that eventually exhaustion and malnutrition would no longer render them useful to the government's frantic arms race. The Jews of Berlin lived with the inescapable knowledge that the fires of November ninth were indeed the couriers of greater evils to follow.

We watched with a mounting sense of helplessness the disappearance of people from our midst and spoke of their possible fate, so closely linked to our own, in hushed voices, stunned by the general conspiracy of silence that allowed these things to happen. We did not know how to interpret this silence, whether its genesis was one of intimidation or complicity. Our own silence was equivalent to an admission of powerlessness against the perpetrators; yet, the very knowledge of our limitations in the face of absolute power fostered in us a tenacious resolve to frustrate their plans for our extinction by thinking only of our survival. That resolve, its roots more spiritual perhaps, resulted in numerous practical actions in accordance with the needs of the moment. The most sustaining defense we had against the vicious defamations and degradations of our people was the belief in our worth as human beings and our pride in the many accomplishments of Jewish men and women of the past. This belief never wavered, especially when confronted with the fierce rhetoric of Hitler and Goebbels, inflaming the behavior of those who acted on it. We questioned how much the people around us, on the streets, on the trains, going to school or work, those silent, passive ones, knew what was happening to us, their Jewish compatriots. What did they think as they looked past the yellow stars, past those carrying their meager belongings to the collection centers, or past Jews being loaded onto trains? Did they think, did they care at all? Unless non-Jews like Frau Schmidt or my father's friends Helmut and Rudi openly expressed their repugnance for the dehumanization of fellow citizens, the minds and hearts of the silent majority were closed to us, like confidential files stacked against us.

It was still summer. Jewish schools had been permanently closed and the beginning of our forced labor was two weeks away. A few more sun-drenched days were ours to do whatever we wanted in the secluded corners of our homes where the yellow star disappeared into some drawer, to help us forget our present status.

Walking to Mira's house, the gilded leaves on the trees and the warm breezes touching my skin restored my old faith that life can be good, that nature ignores the false barriers set up by humans for other human beings and bestows her bounties indiscriminately.

During our meetings, Mira and I avoid talking about the inevitable yet uncertain future for as long as possible. We cling instead to what we know best; the memory of friends no longer with us, the squabbles we had with teachers, the boys we liked and those we mocked, the dreams we shared. Because talking about absent friends inevitably induces sadness, we recall episodes with teachers about which we can still laugh in retrospect.

"Remember our music teacher, Mr. Solomon?" We would remind each other, and then list one comic incident after another. "We were pretty cruel at times in teasing him, remember?" And we recall the image of a pitiably short man with balding head, watery blue eyes slightly red around the edges, and a pasty complexion that was the token of a secluded, indoor life. He could not conceal his love of Mozart even when we tried to deride his enthusiasm with our unruly behavior. We started to laugh again when we remembered how the class would deliberately sing the wrong notes every time we saw him struggle with teaching us to sing the *Knabenchor* from Mozart's *Zauberflöte*.

"That made him wild with anger and frustration," Mira smiled at the recollection. "We enjoyed making him mad and watching his face grow red, his arms waving in helpless desperation. We pretended we were tone deaf and he believed us. But he tried over and over to make musicians out of us."

"Yes," I concurred, "and that only added to our resistance. He used to scream at us when nothing else worked and I remember one sentence in particular, 'It would be easier to teach cows to sing than you kids.' Now he may be in some camp singing his beloved Mozart to himself. Poor man."

Other teachers who had made an impact stood out as well. Direktor Dr. Schwarz, for example, never let us forget that he was a Doctor of Philosophy and insisted on being addressed as *Herr Doktor*. He had seen better days before circumstances forced him to teach a bunch of wayward *Volksschüler*, elementary public-school students. His preferred disciplinary measure was to rap our knuckles with a ruler and then justify his actions with an oft-repeated phrase, *Wie es in den Wald hineinschallt, so schallt es heraus* (what goes around comes around). He also was a short, rotund and balding man in his fifties who earned our complete disdain with his bragging and show of superiority. And then there was Doktor Rubenstein, also an elderly, portly gentleman who had at one time held a more prestigious position but who nevertheless dedicated his energy to imparting some of his vast store of knowledge about history in a gentle and persuasive manner. It was rumored that he committed suicide after he had received his notice for deportation.

At the mention of that word, we were back in the present reality of our impending forced labor. It also reminded me of something I had not yet told Mira.

"Vera came by two days ago to say goodbye." I waited for Mira's response. She gave me a startled look and then asked me what seemed a perfectly logical question.

"Where is she going?" But then, catching herself in time, in a voice changed to a mere whisper, she said, "Oh," expecting me to tell her more. I told her the rest.

Vera's family had received the notice for their resettlement to Theresienstadt the day before, including a list of things they were allowed to take with them. They were being sent to that camp because her father had been a well-known attorney and the camp was reserved mainly for elderly and prominent Jews. One of her brothers had left earlier on a Kindertransport to England, the other had to go with his parents and Vera. She stayed for only minutes, spent for the most part in an awkward, painful silence, afraid to consider, much less give voice to the grimmest of possibilities. If she was frightened at all, it did not show, instead she said, with the suggestion of a smile, "Let's say *Auf Wiedersehen* as though we mean it." There was a last embrace – no words, no tears – we parted as though she were going on a long vacation.

Mira and I were quiet for a while, following our own thoughts, and then, afraid to voice our deeper fears, we wondered aloud what our first day at the ammunition factory would have in store for us.

The alarm went off at five a.m. Awake but disoriented, I had a strong inclination to stay in bed for another few minutes when a sudden thought made me sit bolt upright and jump out of bed. My heart started to beat twice as fast when I remembered that being late for work was considered sabotage, punishable by immediate deportation, no questions asked.

I dressed quickly and went into the kitchen where my father was preparing breakfast, such as it was - a slice of mushy black bread with just a hint of margarine and a cup of hot "*Ersatzkaffee*" that gave the illusion of dispelling sleepiness. Since my mother stayed up late to wash or mend our work clothes, she got up later in the morning and had her breakfast with

Hans. My father was making my lunch which, on ordinary days, consisted of the same mushy bread with some margarine on it, but on better days, like that morning, of a piece of cheese he had pilfered. My father rationed the cheese carefully and, whether the portion turned out small or large, we always thought of those days as feast days because it made the bread palatable. Looking at the slices of the bread, I had difficulty imagining how the grain of the earth could turn into such a mess of rubbery mush. We often suspected and probably came close to the truth, that less wholesome ingredients, like sawdust, were added to it to expand its consumption.

My father and I made some drowsy overtures at conversation during which he did most of the talking, giving me advice on how to conduct myself in the workplace, how to relate to my non-Jewish co-workers and superiors, and to be sure that I had all the necessary papers with me, especially the travel permit that allowed me to use the elevated train to and from work. He reiterated what he had been telling us so often of his own experiences and impressions as a forced laborer himself. Many if not most of his non-Jewish co-workers, simple working class people, were anti-Nazis who had been associated with the Socialist or Communist parties in this country before 1933. There were a few among them who had joined the NSDAP to secure their promotion but who were not necessarily anti-Semitic. His final caution, as always, was not to trust anyone except the people closest to you who had proven true in the past, because *Die Zeiten sind zu unsicher*, times are too uncertain.

Our conversation switched easily to the previous night's air raid, a particularly long and frightening one, an example of how life could be cut off in seconds. Talking about these nightly terrors always quelled the unease they left behind because we could share our relief at having survived another attack. Our talk then turned to our places of work and, as so often in the past, we wished that the Allied planes would hit more crucial targets than civilian homes, such as the railroad stations or factories where Jews were doing forced labor, which would have been empty in the dead of night. We knew it was a pipe dream because, unless it resulted in a total defeat of Germany and an end to the persecution of Jews, the Allied bombardment of German cities incited the Hitlerites' anger against Jews all the more.

I left the house early enough to be able to arrive at the factory fifteen minutes before seven as ordered. I joined the darkness outside and disappeared into the sleeping city, still suffused with the lingering smell of burnt-out buildings. Feeling protected by the blackout, I covered the yellow star and relished my anonymity for as long as the night would hide my true identity. I had taken to doing this reckless concealment whenever I felt safe from detection. Covering the yellow star gave me an unaccustomed thrill of daring and the momentary exhilaration of being free of this stigma.

On the first day of work at the ammunition factory, Mira and I met at the Charlottenburg train station. It felt good to have each other's company, although we found it difficult to express our feelings of anxiety. Fear of the unknown kept our lips sealed and instead gave way to introspection where the mind dwells on images rather than words. The silence between us was broken only when we mentioned some trivia or other.

After getting off at Steglitz station, we had no difficulty locating the factory, some distance away. As required by the notice sent to us, we went directly to the general manager's office to report for work. A tall, handsome man in his early forties, with brown eyes and brown hair, greeted us cordially and with a slightly accented *Guten Morgen* instead of the customary *Heil Hitler*, prompted most likely by looking at our yellow stars. A good omen, as it turned out. He introduced himself as Herr Sorensen. He was the owner of the factory and a native of Sweden, another sign in our favor. Herr Sorensen checked our papers and then gave us a long and puzzled look, the expression caught between a frown and a smile.

"You are only fourteen," he said, more as a question than a statement of fact, looking directly at me. Mira was a year older. I expected him to raise objections for having to employ girls so young in his business of supplying material for the war, watched over by men from the SS and the Gestapo.

"I'll be fifteen in a few months," I said eagerly, anxious to assert the truth to fend off rejection because of my age. For, if I could not be of any use to the Third Reich... then what?

"Well," he said finally, with an indulgent smile at listening to my unspoken plea, "follow me."

He led us to a large room, astir with the pounding of heavy machinery at which two men were working already. He called one of them to where we were standing.

"Herr Wegner, will you instruct these girls in the use of the machines? They're going to be working for me."

His request was curt and formal. Then, with a nod of his head, he left us under the supervision of Herr Wegner from that day on. Because of our addition to the work force, Herr Wegner had earned a promotion to foreman. He was of medium stature, with ash blond hair and pale blue eyes and my initial impression was that he treated us with detached civility. Looking us straight in the eyes rather than at our yellow stars, he motioned us to follow him to one of the machines. Mira was first to get instructions on how to operate a drilling machine, which I had to watch carefully in case I would use it some day. He cautioned us against making possible mistakes and what their consequences might be, either to ourselves or to those using the final product. As a living example of what might result if we were careless, he pointed to the man across from us who was already at work on a monstrously large machine that made a combination of gigantic thumping and hissing noises. Herr Wegner told us that the man had lost a finger at the drilling machine a couple of years ago because his hand had slipped and was trapped in the drill. Mira and I looked at each other while I stopped breathing momentarily. He asked Mira to sit at the machine and drill a hole into the flat, square end of a screw as long as her hand. She did so with amazing ease and Herr Wegner acknowledged her success with a faint smile of both approval and relief. After another successful attempt, he motioned me to follow him.

He took me to a machine that was separated from Mira's by a wide column that blocked our view, though Mira and I sat facing each other. My job was to stamp out curious shapes from a thin metal sheet about four feet long and six inches wide. The sheet was so sharp that by the end of the day the inside of my right hand, with which I had to push the sheet through the machine, was cut and swollen by the time I reached home. That night my mother put Vaseline and a bandage around it to speed the healing process. The following morning my hand felt stiff and my mother gave me another bandage to wrap around my hand once I got to work. "We'll have to get you a pair of gloves," she said reassuringly.

For most of the day the cloth around my hand afforded me some protection from the sharp edges of the metal, but before the day was over, I had to ask Herr Wegner for another piece of cloth. He readily provided me with one and I felt assured of his concern. After all, I had now entered service for the Reich.

That night, when I got home, my mother was worried that my hand might get infected and repeated the procedure from the night before. She also gave me an old pair of her leather gloves.

"Use the right one first and when that wears out use the left one. They may last a week, by then I might be able to get you a better pair."

She was right - they did last me a little over a week before they too were torn to shreds. My grandfather was finally able to procure me a pair of leather gloves from one of his co-workers. They seemed custom-made for work like mine, and I soon became an expert on the stamping machine.

The days passed in dreary monotony. Our sleep at night was punctured by the sound of sirens warning us to seek shelter in our cellars, and the droning of the British planes overhead alerted us to the detonation of bombs soon to follow. The lights going off in our cellar were a signal of a close-by hit and we waited with bodies tensed in anticipation of our house being next.

My world during the day was filled with the sound of metal pounding on metal and at night metal pounding on stone. In all this cacophony, the gentler sounds of the human voice grew ever fainter, like the last bars of a beautiful song.

The days were growing shorter, colder, darker, until I thought I would never see the sun again. It was dark when I left the house for work after 6 a.m. and it was dark when I returned after 7 p.m. The grimy, oil-stained windows of our room in the factory only teasingly admitted sparse rays of sunlight in rare moments when the sun peeped through the clouds. The sky was overcast most of the time with muddy colored, low-lying clouds and smoke from bombed-out buildings; the wind sprayed the city with a fine, wet, black dust that stung the eyes. The stench of burning buildings, mingled with that of human flesh, never quite left the air we breathed.

Now that winter had begun, getting out of bed in the icy air of an un-heated room felt like the most merciless part of the day. Overcoming those first moments of the body's temperature adjusting to the cold, while still drugged with sleep and exhaustion, became a gigantic feat for me. Each night I went to bed thinking I could not face another dawn, each morning I scored another victory over my body's resistance.

There was no heat in our factory, and the problem of dressing warmly during the winter months presented a constant challenge for my mother, since Jews received no ration cards for textiles. She rummaged through the discarded clothes of her sister, her two cousins, and asked acquaintances for warm sweaters to be worn under my cotton smock. At times it helped me to think of those trapped in the work camps whose lot I imagined to be a hundred times worse than mine.

One day Herr Wegner assigned me to file some pieces to make them fit into batteries to be assembled. He had warned me earlier that the slightest deviation from the amount to be filed down could result in serious dam-age to the battery. Each time I finished a piece, he took it to some corner of the room where I saw him put it into an object of undefined form. As the hours passed, I could feel the lack of sleep. The concentrated effort I had to spend on each piece wearied my eyes even more and slackened my grip in hands numb with cold. What I feared all along finally happened.

Herr Wegner had just taken another piece when I heard his voice from the other end of the room shouting, out of control.

"Damn Jew! Haven't I told you to be careful? Look what you've done."

At that, I turned around and saw him coming towards me with one arm raised high, holding a hammer, while in the other he was holding the piece I had just worked on. His face distorted with anger as he continued walking towards me. I looked at him, then at the hammer, with only one thought; he won't... he can't...

Suddenly, I seemed to be no longer in the factory. Herr Wegner was no longer just an individual, my supervisor, but the accumulation of all we had to endure from non-Jews. The raised arm with the hammer was no longer just his, it became the image for all the arms raised in salute to the man whose threats were hanging like the shadow of death over our heads. I heard myself crying out loud in a voice I did not recognize, which changed into one lone and breathless wailing that engulfed me in a deep, soft darkness.

When I came to, I was lying on the cold cement floor, my head in someone's lap, aware of whispers coming from different sides. I had no recollection of how I had gotten into this position but soon recognized the faces bending over me. My head was lying in Mira's lap. Herr Sorensen was looking at me with eyes round with concern. Other workers had gathered as well, including Herr Wegner looking rather sheepishly at the scene he had caused. Mira, seeing my confusion, told me what had happened.

"You were screaming so loudly that everybody thought immediately you'd had a serious accident and came rushing in to find out. You fainted and were out for a while. How do you feel now?"

"Fine," I answered her, surprised and pleased at the attention I was getting all of a sudden, but also afraid of having caused resentment for interrupting everyone's work. Yet the concern and reassurances I received helped me relax and when Herr Wegner, by way of apology, told me later that he never intended to strike me in earnest, I knew that here, in this place at least, I was regarded as a human being. Herr Wegner concluded this episode with a reminder, "Just don't let it happen again or it may cost someone's life, and I don't mean only yours."

For the first time in all the weeks I had been working at the factory, I was made aware of the responsibility placed upon me and the consequences if I failed carrying it out. That evening I told my parents the events of the day and we discussed the tragic irony of Jews being forced to be involuntary contributors to a war we all hated, that gave license to the murder of innocent lives. Yet we knew that a possible attempt at sabotage would imperil our own lives and those of family members even more. We had no choice but to be agents of our own destruction, whether we complied or resisted. We placed our hope in those nightly visitors from the sky to balance the scales of justice, even if we might not live long enough to celebrate their victory.

Our lunch break was thirty minutes long. During that time, Jewish workers were allowed to visit with each other. Mira preferred to have that time alone with me since there was now so little time for socializing. But, whenever I saw a chance to escape her possessiveness, I went to another, smaller room in the factory where a few Jewish workers were sitting behind long work tables, assembling pieces to be used in the batteries. That room was without the incessant pounding of machines that canceled out all thoughts. A girl I had barely known in school was working at one of the tables and, always conscious of the vagaries of time, we soon became close friends. Her name was Steffi Blumenthal. She had been a year ahead of me in school and had recently been transferred to our factory from one that had been bombed.

Mira reacted in her predictable way to this new friendship and kept herself aloof much of the time from Steffi. The few occasions she did join us for lunch she spent looking sullen and hurt whenever Steffi and I could not hide the pleasure we took in each other's company. I put my feelings on ice as I watched Mira's sullen withdrawal from attempts we made to include her in our partnership. No amount of coaxing, reasoning, or arguing with Mira could persuade her how much I valued both friendships, that I could not and would not relinquish one for the other, if that was a choice she expected me to make.

It was not until Steffi made repeated overtures of friendship that Mira relented somewhat and responded positively to Steffi's genuine interest in her. Indeed, no one could for long resist being drawn into the magic circle of Steffi's warm personality, so obvious in her lively brown eyes, her gentle, somewhat tentative smile, and soft voice. Those were the quiet times that brought solace to our daily hardships and we shouldered our burden together by talking or remembering old jokes or incidents from school. They did not, however, prevent the occurrence of relapses when Mira, overcome with distrust like water breaking through a dam, would deluge me with accusations of trying to abandon her for another friend, asserting that I had never been her true friend. One day she persisted in her irrational rage until I, bereft of words to calm her fears, turned from her with a despondent shrug of the shoulders and told her, "You are the one destroying our friendship." I left her standing alone with her unprovoked rancor and her pain. At times like these, I despaired of being able to continue my friendship with her.

Mira did not come to work the day after our fight and I knew the reason for her absence. I explained to Steffi that emotional upheavals frequently brought on epileptic seizures, that Mira felt particularly vulnerable after she had lived through another battle with me when she thought herself rejected. To Steffi's question of what had brought on our last argument, I told her that it was about the book Steffi had given me for my fifteenth birthday a month ago. Steffi listened, and the expression on her face changed from puzzlement to sympathetic understanding so that, in the end, compassion won out over resentment and we decided to be more careful in the future not to incite Mira's anger.

"After all, no one knows how much longer we'll have each other," we agreed.

Sitting at my machine after lunch, I thought of Mira at home, imprisoned in a body that had so few defenses against the anguish of her heart. Perhaps she was more fragile than the rest of us; though her turmoil was also mine and that of others, her struggling body making visible what lay hidden in our minds.

———

The days passed in an endless succession of meaningless tasks that faded into nothingness. We never saw the sum total of what we had to produce during the eleven hours spent amidst the rhythmic pounding and crashing of machines. My ears had grown so accustomed to the incessant noise that my mother had to remind me I need not shout when talking to her at home.

One day, while Mira and I were working on the machines to which we had originally been assigned, I heard a less familiar sound, a piercing, urgent scream coming from Mira's direction. "Turn off the machine!" I heard another voice, coming from the man with the missing finger who sat across from us and who had spotted the trouble instantly. We both jumped up and, since I was closer to the switch, I turned it off and the screaming subsided. He and I approached Mira's machine at the same moment. She was sitting with her head down to one side of the drill, her hair was caught in it, and below it lay the screw she had tried to retrieve. We managed to gently disentangle her hair from the drill and only then saw the damage it had done. There was an open wound on top of her head, the size of a silver dollar, where the drill had torn out her hair.

Herr Sorenson had heard Mira scream as well and came running into the room to investigate its source. Concern was written all over his face and he asked me to take Mira to the nurse's office. Mira winced from the pain that the boric acid of the drill added to that of the open wound. The nurse was sympathetic and treated Mira with efficient care, then comforted her by telling her she should stay home a day or two to allow for the healing. Mira followed her advice, and when she returned two days later, she told me that she had had an epileptic seizure that same night. She added that the accident had been her fault because she had been told to turn off the drill in an emergency.

"I guess I learned my lesson," she said.

What a lousy way to learn a lesson, I thought with some bitterness at making a fifteen-year-old girl work at this devilish machine.

———

Long before we make actual contact, I feel his presence beside me, inspecting my work at the filing machine. He moves slightly closer and is standing so close to me that I can feel his breath on my neck. Without looking at him, I sense some dark, nameless danger coming from his person and know what a cornered animal must feel like when set upon by its hunter. He starts to speak in a voice lowered to a sinuous whisper and, though his words are commonplace, even trite, they sting me with their sexual nuances. I had never been spoken to like this before, but some inborn knowledge tells me that this is the language of the male in pursuit of the female.

"You handle this machine very well," I hear him say, but know he means something else, though what it might be I dare not admit to myself and am at a loss how to respond. A furtive glance out of the corner of my eye confirms what I feared all along. It is a young SS officer, strangely at odds with his surroundings in his immaculate uniform, smelling of expensive soap or aftershave lotion, and acting as though he had no care in the world other than flirting with a Jewish girl. Or has he not seen the yellow star?

He compliments me again on my dexterity, my youth, and the daintiness of my hands.

"Much too dainty for such harsh work," his voice nearly breathless, sending a cold shudder through me.

What am I to do? He has obviously not seen my yellow star, I conclude, standing, as he is, on my right side. He would be enraged if he discovered that he had been flirting with a Jewess. I have to tell him, I decide, and thus, slowly and deliberately, I turn to face him so that he can see the yellow patch against my black smock, rising from it like a bright star in the night sky.

"Had you not noticed this?" I ask, no longer afraid.

"I have," he answers, just as calmly and with a grin on his face. "But it doesn't matter to me. You are very pretty... you don't look Jewish at all... blond hair, gray-green eyes. Are you really a Jewess?"

"Yes, and Hitler certainly thinks so. He would not like to see you talking to me like this," I say, emboldened by his flattery, yet impelled more by fear of being accused of encouraging it. He smiles at my audacity and shrugs his shoulders.

"Probably not," he says finally, "and so it's a good thing he is not all-seeing too. *Tja*, keep up the good work for the Reich. *Heil Hitler!*" With that he straightens up to leave me, taking my fear with him.

"Have you ever been in love?" Steffi asks me during one lunch break.

"Not really," I readily admit. "In fifth grade I had a crush on a boy who was in my class. We never even talked to each other, but just exchanged shy and embarrassed glances and written notes. After him I thought most boys were silly and awkward. Mira and I often fantasized about meeting the ideal boy, what qualities and looks he would have to have. How about you?"

"When I was fourteen I fell seriously in love with a boy and he with me. We compared ourselves to the famous pair, Romeo and Juliet. We soon became close friends who talked about getting married sometime in the future. But then, a year later, soon after we graduated, he left for Palestine to join a kibbutz. We wrote letters to each other for as long as it was permitted. Now we have lost contact and I don't know whether we will ever be able to resume our friendship. It makes me sad."

I share her regrets but at the same time have to admit to myself that I envy her for this short-lived romance. From that day on I regard her more as a woman than a mere *Backfisch*, a dreamy teenager like myself.

Steffi is gone. She had not come to work for nearly a week and I finally gather enough courage to ask the owner of the factory, Herr Sorensen, a Swede, to hear the worst. The look in his eyes confirms my premonition. He remains silent for a while before speaking haltingly.

"The Gestapo informed me... they told me... the Blumenthal family will be relocated... they are needed somewhere else. I am so sorry." His voice is shaking, and he is barely able to conceal his feelings before he turns abruptly to leave.

I cannot move from the spot at first. Steffi... my good friend Steffi... dear, gentle Steffi. Relocated... needed somewhere else. Where? For what end? It's all a big lie, a horrible, cruel lie.

I sit down at my machine again, hardly aware of what my body is doing. Everything is blurry. I let the tears run freely down my cheeks. Let the whole world see them. I want to scream, howl, hide, anything but do this meaningless work for this confounded war, for these hated robbers of everything I treasure. So many had already disappeared without a good-bye.

Who will be next?

What will happen to all of them?

Tante Helene, Onkel Hugo, Vera, Rita Orbach... ? And now Steffi... There is little refuge in tears, for Jewish tears have been banned from this land of iron hearts.

There is no longer any refuge in prayer, for God seems to have gone deaf.

I cannot eat my lunch, meager as it is. My throat feels trapped in a tight clasp. I give my sandwich to Mira who eats it with relish because a piece of smooth buttery cheese hides between the two slices of mushy black bread. How we hold on to life despite the destruction all around us. My thoughts are with Steffi, and even Mira shares in my sorrow as we whisper a last *Auf Wiedersehen*, Steffi, with just the faintest hope to meet again.

The clock reads two minutes to seven on the morning of February 27, 1943 when I sit down at my machine to start work. Mira's place is empty. When the clock shows two minutes after seven, I know she will not be coming to work. Her epileptic seizures had increased after her accident at the drilling machine. She dreads it, yet dares not refuse her assignment to it.

The familiar noise of machines running soon fills the room. Moments later another sound rises above the clanging of metal against metal and I hear, what up to now I had only seen scrawled on walls and posters, "*Juden Raus!*" I look up from my work and see the room filling with armed SS men, while trailing behind them are the remaining Jewish workers who look bewildered but resigned, as though they had expected this for a long time. I get up from my stool to join the group, my mind empty of all thought.

Herr Sorensen comes into the room with quickened steps, his face mirroring his indignation and agitation. I see him address one of the SS men, speaking to him with great insistence, and I feel sure he is trying to voice his opposition to this intrusion into his factory and its daily routine. There is a brief exchange between the two men and the expression on Herr Sorensen's face changes from open challenge to reluctant compliance. His eyes fasten on us, as if wanting to speak through them all that is in his heart. I look at my co-workers and see written in their faces the same, undisguised feeling of alarm and helplessness. We stand like statues, until another order of "*Raus!*" shakes us out of our trance, and we follow the men into the front yard where a truck is waiting for us. Herr Sorensen's *Kommt bald wieder*, "come back soon," echoes in my ears as we climb into the truck as ordered. That is the first time I notice his Swedish accent.

The canvas is lowered, no doubt to shield us from the view of our fellow citizens. Losing contact with the outside world confirms my first fears about our destination. The lowered canvas is proof to me of the bad conscience of our abductors.

Driving for a while through the quiet morning hours, I am seized with an unnameable dread that finds relief in a whisper to the woman sitting next to me, "They're going to kill us. They're going to set the truck on fire."

"*Aber nein, nein,*" she whispers in return, patting my arm for added reassurance. "They won't do that in the middle of the city. Be brave... don't let them know you're afraid... it makes them angrier."

As long as I can hear the early morning traffic, my fears dissipate somewhat and change to anxious curiosity. My thoughts are with my family, with my mother especially, who would be exempt from sharing the same fate as her family. I dare not think it to the end.

Before long the truck comes to a stop. The canvas is drawn aside and what presents itself to my view makes me hesitate to leave the truck that only minutes ago had seemed the deadliest place on earth, but which now feels like a haven. Outside, gathered in a small courtyard, are hoards of armed SS men with death's-heads on their caps staring at us with a sinister glare. The familiar bellowing of "*Raus! Raus! Schnell machen,*" sets my body in motion as though obeying some electrical impulse.

Having been the last one to get on the truck, I am the first one to step off into a grey-green wave of uncertainty.

I try to walk with firm steps between two rows of SS men toward the entrance of a building I do not recognize. Passing the guards on both sides of me, I can almost feel the bullet in my back. I feel safe only after I enter the interior of the building where more SS men see to it that everything is going according to plan. A few yellow stars have already arrived and all is quiet, except for the shouting of orders. Men are ordered to go to the right, women to the left. We are forbidden to speak when in the presence of the SS.

Once I find myself among the women who had already been brought, my fear leaves me like an ill-fitting garment. I ask one of them whether she knows where we are.

"No idea," she shrugs her shoulders. "And it doesn't really matter, because we're all headed in the same direction."

I leave her, trying to find more cheerful company.

We wait.

It is almost ten in the morning. Isolated shouts of "*Schnell, schnell,*" tell us that another transport has arrived. More women join us.

We wait.

There is no food, no water. We had not been allowed to take our lunches with us and my stomach tells me that it must be past lunchtime. Other concerns, however, supersede the feeling of hunger. We talk little among ourselves since everyone is anxious to avoid speaking of what lies closest to our hearts: the fate of our families.

We wait.

As the minutes and the hours pass, some women arrive with scraps of information about what seems to be happening all over the city. Military trucks are collecting Jews from their workplaces and from their homes. People are beaten for refusing to cooperate or for not being fast enough, which is true for most of the elderly and the sick. One woman had seen a truck unloading an older and a younger woman whose faces were streaming with blood. After them followed a man whose leg had been injured as he hobbled off the truck. The faces of the others, she tells us, had turned into masks stiff with terror.

We wait.

More and more arrive. There must have been hundreds by mid-afternoon. Among the new arrivals is a woman who recognizes the place from the time her-husband-to-be had brought her to dances and musical entertainments. The building we are in is called "Clou," and, at the mention of the name, I remember stories my father told us of better days spent here.

A curious calm hangs over everything. There is no panic. No one is crying or losing control. People try to comfort each other with the hope that they will be reunited with their family members at some point during the massive round-up. A sudden shriek breaks the calm, a woman's voice, then another, followed by coarse and angry commands from an SS man. There is absolute silence throughout the hall. No one has to explain to us the cause of those screams. Some poor wretch, perhaps a feeble old woman, had not moved fast enough and had aroused the indignation and sadism of an SS man. More than ever we feel bonded by a common dread and repugnance of our ruthless adversaries.

We wait.

Some women had decided to flush whatever valuables they had down the toilet rather than hand them over to the SS. Most jewelry had been confiscated long before this day and what was left were wedding rings, small necklaces or cheap watches, trinkets all, including some currency for train fares.

"You don't need to do this," one woman advises me, who had heard me talk of my family.

"Why not?" I want to know.

"Because you'll be able to go home again."

"What makes you so sure of that?"

"They're not deporting '*Mischlinge*' as yet."

"I'm not a *Mischling*... I've been declared a *Geltungsjüdin* by the Nuremberg Laws."

"Yes, but your mother is considered an 'Aryan.' They won't deport children of 'Aryans' because they're afraid of repercussions."

"My mother is also Jewish," I answer her, feeling defensive and angry at hearing my mother labeled with the hated word "Aryan." Arguments with Mira and other classmates about my mixed origin surface in my memory and, at that moment, I fear exclusion more than the possibility of death. I feel ready, almost anxious, to die with these women if that is going to be their destiny. But then I think of my parents and brother, what they must be going through, alone or together, and whether I would ever see them again. The thought of my mother's anguish especially, mirrored in the faces of these women, separated from their husbands and children, confronts me with the selfishness of my wishful thinking and I am left in conflict.

A flurry of motion breaks the spell of waiting. Names are being called, and those called go down the steps and do not return. The SS seem to follow an alphabetical order and the crowd of women around me is thinning out fast, like the unloading of a truck full of goods. It is past dinnertime but no one complains of hunger. Around ten in the evening I hear my name coming from a distance, but loud and clear. I follow the direction of the sound and see a long line of women waiting behind a row of tables where SS men are sitting with piles of papers in front of them. Across from our line is the men's line, the men darting furtive glances at the women to see whether a wife, a daughter, a sister, or other relatives may be among them. Everything proceeds with bureaucratic efficiency and in complete silence. Talk is prohibited. Guards with guns slung over their shoulders serve as deterrents.

Most of the people whose papers had been checked are ordered to go to the left, through a door opposite the one we had entered. A wave of the hand and a short *"Raus!"* seals their doom - irrevocably. I watch it all with the calm detachment of an observer and expect to go with them through that exit from which there is no return. I know that, not as one knows a fact, but as one knows that the distant roaring of the wind will bring a hurricane.

A young woman just ahead of me is being questioned and, after a short pause, is sent to the right, the first one so far. As she turns to pass me, I notice her blond hair, blue eyes, and that she must be in her early twenties. This could not possibly happen twice, I think, as I wait for my turn. I am taking her place in line while an SS man searches through my papers. Without looking up, he begins to question me.

"Name?"

"Rita Sara Kuhn."

"Age?"

"Fifteen years."

"Address?"

"Berlin-Charlottenburg, Sybelstrasse 62."

"Father's name?

"Fritz Israel Kuhn."

"Address?"

"Berlin-Charlottenburg, Sybelstrasse 62."

"Mother's name?"

"Frieda Kuhn."

"Maiden name?"

"Krüger."

"Address?"

"Berlin-Charlottenburg, Sybelstrasse 62."

There is a brief pause while he checks the papers again. Then, still not looking at me, he waves his hand and says gruffly, *"Nach rechts."* He must have made a mistake. I do not move. A sharp, impatient, *"Raus!* Go home," makes me turn to leave the hall, still expecting to be called back. When nothing happens, I quicken my steps to find myself enveloped in total darkness on the street where a voice from a lone figure welcomes me with, "Thank God, someone else is leaving this place." I recognize the young woman who had been released before me. We find obvious relief in each other's company, both equally puzzled about our location or where the nearest subway station might be. We walk together in the same direction until we come to a sign saying "U" and head down the stairs to the underground train. Since we have restricted travel permits, we agree it would be safer to hide our yellow stars so as not to run the risk of being picked up by prowling SS men looking to arrest more Jews. The mention of our families never passes our lips, though they are more than ever in my thoughts. Would they be waiting for me at home or...?

It is late, close to midnight.

Entering the compartment of the train, I have a strange experience. My body feels as though it were no longer a part of me and I look at everything as a traveler from another continent, even another planet, might look at the scene before me. It is an ordinary sight on most days, but at this moment it takes on a different dimension. I look at the passengers sitting huddled in their winter coats, their scarves, their thoughts, their sleep, as though they were a group of sculptures from a museum. I want to shake them out of their torpor. Shout at them, scream at them: don't you know what is happening in your city? How can you be so indifferent? How can you go about your own business, when there are thousands and thousands of people sent to their death? Mothers separated from their small children...?

Getting off the train, I feel weighed down with a terrible knowledge while they... while they sit there wrapped in their deadly ignorance. Who is better off I cannot tell.

———

I go up the stairs to our second-floor apartment and slow my steps the closer I come to it. Will they be home? Standing before the familiar door it seems as though I had been away for a long time since I left it that morning. A few seconds pass before I ring the doorbell and when I do I involuntarily hold my breath to stop feeling anything.

Frau Schmidt opens the door after the second ring and cannot say anything at first, looking much like someone who is seeing a ghost. The question that is burning in my mind must have shown in my eyes, for suddenly her voice returns to her and she cries out, "Ritachen," loud enough for anyone in the apartment to hear. Indeed, it does not take long until I see my father, mother, and Hans come out of the kitchen door, white with fright but managing a smile of relief. My father is the first to reach me and collapses on my shoulder, trembling with joy and muttering repeatedly, "*Püppchen, ach, mein Püppchen.*" My mother and brother embrace me next and we all go into the living room where they urge me to tell the day's events, but not before giving me my first meal of the day.

I have some difficulty reciprocating their joy. The images of families torn apart are still too vivid and will not yield to the reunion taking place at that moment. I left part of myself in that huge hall of misery and silent tears, and the smiles that greet my return feel like a desecration of all the tragedies happening that day. And yet I am glad at my family's sense of relief that the doorbell ringing that late announced my return rather than the Gestapo's arrival.

Sleep does not come easily this night, nor do tears. Something died within me in that huge hall, something dark and heavy had taken its place and I feel boxed in, as though buried alive. I try to pray, but the words are lost.

Only one wish is haunting me, "Please, God, do not spare me...do not spare me..." and with that I fall asleep.

And then they came for us...

A week had passed since my arrest. Neither my father nor I were called back to work, which filled us with unease. We knew of the labor shortage and that every worker was needed for intensifying the war effort to compensate for the losses in the East. It was an ominous sign that we had not been called back to forced labor.

On March 5th, a Friday, my mother went to pick up our ration cards at a school nearby. She left early that day but, contrary to our expectations, returned soon after. As she entered the door, something in her demeanor held us locked in fear. Her lips were shut like a sealed tomb; her eyes avoided looking at us directly and when she finally spoke her voice sounded hollow, as though it had become the mouthpiece of some higher order.

"They wouldn't give them to me. You have to go get them yourselves," she said, with her eyes still averted.

"That's it," my father said in response to the news, his voice remarkably clear and steady. "Put on some extra layers of clothes." That was all the advice he gave us and there was no need for an explanation. How many Jewish parents had told their children the same thing before having to leave their home?

The four of us set out for the school. Once inside, my mother directed us to a room with several SS men in it, some standing, some seated behind tables with papers piled before them which they examined with granite faces. Robots, I thought. Nothing human can penetrate these iron masks. It all seemed terribly familiar to me and I knew what the procedure would be. They asked us questions and checked our answers with the papers stacked in front of them. These contained our vital statistics. And that was what we were to these men - mere statistics, living or dead. They did not acknowledge us with a glance. It was all the same to them. They were automatons, set in motion by an invisible mastermind, performing their function with cold and impenetrable regularity. After our papers were checked, the SS man sitting behind the desk snapped an order to another standing near us, "Take them away."

My mother made ready to join us as we followed the SS man, but he brushed her away with a brusque, "No! Not you!" Her face changed color, looking ashen and rigid, her arms dropped helplessly to her side. The look in her eyes, full of non-comprehension and deep pain, followed me into the room which became our prison, and remain with me ever after. The key turned in the lock with a finality that brooked no dissension, no reversal. Without a word, we sat down on the classroom chairs, connected by a fearful knowledge that took refuge in silence.

Images began rushing through my mind of people being loaded onto trucks, men and women separated, the hushed talk, the feeling of solidarity, the selection to the right or left, and I wondered how long it would be before we were separated and whether this time it would be our turn to go left.

My father broke the silence by saying, "I guess they realized they made a mistake when they released you a week ago, so... our poor Mama," he sighed.

Again, silence. My heart wept.

The key turned in the lock once more to admit more yellow stars, people deceived like us by the necessity of coming to get their ration cards. A Jewish woman, Frau Goedicke, who had recently come to occupy one of our bedrooms, entered at one point with hesitant step and eyes cast to the ground, but as soon as she saw us, she straightened up and gave us a smile of recognition and relief. There was little talk among those assembled, each harbored thoughts for which there were no words.

Time stopped.

We waited for more people to arrive and did not want to think beyond that. I wanted something to break this anxious quietude, this nameless uncertainty.

Suddenly a woman's voice startled us with its piercing, desperate screams, "Let me see my children. You can't take my children from me... let me go with my children." We listened and could not identify the voice until my father turned to Hans and me and said, loud enough for the others to hear, "*Das ist doch unsere Mama*," that is our Mama. There was a stir in the room, for my mother was known to many from helping in my grandmother's store. Her voice, usually low and gentle, never raised even in anger, was stretched beyond recognition by a terror so great it rose above any care for herself as she faced fully armed SS men.

Just as suddenly as it had started, the voice stopped; in its stead there were other voices, hoarse, male voices giving orders.

What had they done to my mother?

I wanted to leave the room to find out. I wanted to see her, touch her, comfort her as much as I needed her comfort.

Some time later the door opened part way and a familiar face scanned the room, until his eyes found us and he nodded ever so slightly. It was our "Onkel" Helmut, unable to conceal the agitation and solicitude showing in his handsome features. When we questioned him later how in the world he had gained access to our room, he told us he knew from Mama where we were and, under the pretext of having opened the wrong door, he was able to ascertain that we were still safe.

Our true and brave friend, his love so strong as to pass through the circle of hate.

Finally, the door swung wide open and a group of SS men entered and ordered everyone to follow them. We were walking in a file of two and were led into the courtyard. There, under a covered archway, my mother was leaning against the stone wall, motionless, her lips closed as if to suppress a scream; the only life about her was in her eyes, which looked at us like those of a wounded deer.

A truck was waiting for us in the middle of the street. The loading proceeded noiselessly and in broad daylight. There was no lack of witnesses. I was the last one to get on and had to sit between two SS men with their guns poised high. We understood that language. I had a good view of the street and, while waiting for the truck to start moving, fastened my eyes on my mother who stood with the other relatives of those on the truck, among them the daughters of Frau Goedicke, her children from her marriage to a non-Jew. My mother had turned to stone from grief at her children being taken from her.

The moment the truck started to move, one of Frau Goedicke's daughters, Herta, cried out, "*Nehmt mich doch auch mit*," take me too, and then collapsed on the pavement. Her mother behind cried out, and I could see her hand stretched out in a futile gesture to catch her falling daughter. Just then the truck turned a corner – leaving a void where my mother had been.

Someone was comforting Frau Goedicke who had begun to moan quietly, muttering all the while, "*Meine Tochter....meine Herta.*" My thoughts were elsewhere, wondering how this could be happening again, and that I might never wake up from this nightmare. Just then I looked at the SS man to my right and saw his face twitch with emotion. His eyes moistened and... and my hand wanted to move to rest on his shoulder. Was I going mad?

The truck came to a stop. Terse orders of "*Raus!*" told us that we had arrived at our destination. Dusk was falling. The cold was penetrating even through our double layers of clothes. A wet bleakness blanketed the place where other Jews had been collected and stood at attention before SS men and Gestapo agents in leather coats who were making selections. I had no idea where we were and dared not ask my father, since speaking was forbidden. Someone on my left mumbled the name Levetzostrasse, and I could make out the presence of a building known to me from pictures as a synagogue.

So they choose houses of prayer from which to send Jews to their death.

My father stood straight and stiffly before a hulk of a man in civilian clothes who bullied him to reveal our identities. "Jude Fritz Israel Kuhn; Tochter Rita Sara Kuhn; Sohn Hans Israel Kuhn," I heard him say with a steady, clear voice, followed by another voice sizzling with contempt, "*Stinkjuden.*"

Echoes of subdued voices could be heard through the descending darkness, interspersed with obscenities which stood in lurid contrast to the stillness all around, like thunder from a cloudless sky. Someone was shoving me, "To the right!" I went, like a child's mechanical toy, in the direction toward another waiting truck where I saw my father and brother.

Thank God, we were together.

We stopped!

Another unfamiliar building and another unloading.

Once inside, the SS were separating men, women, and children after checking everyone's papers. An SS officer, young and handsome, looked at my papers, then at my yellow star, and finally directly at me with a sardonic smile, "You're really Jewish?" to which I responded by pointing to my ID, "Rita Sara Kuhn," afraid to say anything more to this blond poison.

The inside of the building was dark; a musty smell told me it had not been used or aired for some time. It seemed a perfect hiding place for clandestine actions and though my old fears returned, the words of the woman on the truck reminded me to stay calm, not to let them see my fear of them.

A forced laborer with a yellow star took me up a flight of stairs to a room on the second floor. "Stay here," he said curtly in a tired voice and pointed to a straw mattress on the floor. The room was medium sized, lit by a bare bulb which gave out a feeble light. The damp mattresses explained the odor which met me when I entered. I wanted to turn around but knew I couldn't. There was nothing else to sit on so I sat down on the straw sack assigned to me. I could just make out the shape of three women lying on their mattresses opposite mine. One of them sat huddled in a corner to my left, and the other two near a window to my right. My arrival made little impression on them, no one moved and there was no exchange of greeting. Their silence and immobility only added to the gloom and sense of abandonment pervading this place, in sharp contrast to my own state of agitation and need for human contact. I seemed to be no longer in the land of the living and wanted to know how long they had been here, forgotten by the outside world.

Time held no dimension for these women whose bodies seemed locked in the same position as on the day they were thrown in here, like a sack of potatoes carelessly tossed into some corner, left to rot.

Hope had died here.

Once I got used to my surroundings and the silence became increasingly oppressive, my natural curiosity asserted itself and I asked, "Where are we?" The woman to my left answered with, "Rosenstrasse 2-4, the former Jewish *Hilfsverein*," welfare agency. She fell silent again, whether from lack of energy or interest was difficult to say.

Now that I was settled on my mattress and all action had stopped for the time being, the lack of food caught up with me and I asked myself whether there might be something to eat in this tomb. It was certainly time for supper.

The same orderly who had accompanied me to this floor soon appeared with bowls of soup and slices of black bread which he placed unceremoniously on the floor. We each took our portion and I did so eagerly, but my appetite turned to revulsion at the first sight of the contents in the bowl. More to myself than to those in the room, I expressed my disgust with a very definite, "I can't eat this."

"You'd better...," the woman to my left warned me, "because it's all you're going to get in here."

"But it looks like dirty dish water. What's that swimming around in it?" I asked with a slight shudder.

"Well, if you'd rather go hungry..." the woman shrugged and fell quiet again. Another look at the soup convinced me that I'd rather choose hunger than this toxic brew. The piece of bread will have to do, and I broke off small bits of it to make it last longer.

Language too had died here.

The lack of air, warmth, and energy in these languid bodies was not conducive to conversation so that, more than ever, I thought of my family and whether we would ever be together again. Stifled by the silence and the gloom, I asked the more talkative of the women how long she had been in this place. She welcomed this overture to talk and entered into a dialogue with me while the other two, in all probability mother and daughter, maintained their impenetrable silence.

The woman's name was Miriam Jürgens. When I looked puzzled at the odd combination of names, she told me her story. Her husband was an 'Aryan' with whom she had a son who was not raised as a Jew. They divorced some time in 1937 when he decided to join the NSDAP for "professional advancement," he assured her, and not from conviction. "If I'm lucky and they'll consider me *arisch versippt* (kin to an Aryan), they'll send me to Theresienstadt," she said rather indifferently. She had been waiting for their decision all week since she was taken from her factory on the first day of the round-ups, February 27th. Everyone in this building was living in some form of a mixed marriage, she told me. The Gestapo had not yet decided what to do with the different cases. Some had been deported already for reasons Miriam did not know. She then related a most incredible and unique incident that had occurred outside these walls for the entire week she had been confined to this room.

From the first day of the city-wide round-ups, there had been a demonstration, truly a protest, by the Gentile wives and mothers for their Jewish husbands and children interned in Rosenstrasse. They demanded the release of their family members. It started with a small number but soon swelled to a chorus of a few hundred desperate women shouting, "Give us back our men. Give us back our men." She herself could hear those cries through the only window in our room. There were short intermittences when the SS succeeded in dispersing them, but a few hours later, the women would continue, and in increasing numbers. As a result of this protest many prisoners had been released, while others were deported. The logic of that escaped her because of "the crazy nature of the Nuremberg laws."

"And one day, in the middle of the protest," Miriam continued, "the SS officer in charge of this place came into our room and, standing erect and proud, his hand pointing to the window, he told us, 'Do you hear that? These are your relatives. They want you to go home. We are proud of them. *Das ist deutsche Treue* (that is German loyalty).'"

My face must have been riddled with questions, but instead of answering them, she went on to tell me of another incident.

"But that isn't all," she continued. She had heard it from a woman who witnessed another scene when she arrived at Rosenstrasse, and who had since been released. A verbal exchange had taken place between that same SS officer and two men – the Gentile husband of a Jewish woman being held here, and their son. The husband and son were told by the SS officer that this woman, their wife and mother, would be safe if they agreed to take her home to reside with them. The men refused, whereupon the SS officer yelled at them in language usually reserved for Jews. "*Ihr Schweine-hunde!* You don't deserve to be Germans. *Raus mit euch!*" And with that, he threw them out of the door in a fit of rage.

She finished her story with a "*Tja*," and I knew we were thinking along similar lines, pondering this enigma of a man who momentarily placed his avowed value of family loyalty, long honored by Germanic tribes, over his prescribed duty of sending Jews to their deaths. Such inconsistency between morality and depravity could be more frightening than the blank hatred most SS men expressed towards Jews. The elements of unpredictability and incongruity elicited more fear than the behavior we had come to expect from such men.

And then, leaning forward slightly for fear she might be overheard, Miriam whispered audibly enough, "I don't like to think of SS men as being human, but this man, so proud of the German tradition of loyalty to family, extended even to Jews, is too human for my liking."

Her words mirrored my thoughts. I glanced involuntarily at the door to look for eavesdroppers and only then expressed my agreement with her aloud. We continued talking about other subjects with only slight mention of our families until it was time to go to sleep.

Nighttime brought another kind of terror as the sound of sirens announced the approach of British bombers. In response to my customary reaction of jumping out of bed to head for the cellar, I heard Miriam's voice reminding me there was no shelter for those interned here. I lay down again on my mattress and when the first bombs started falling some distance away, I covered my head with the foul-smelling horse blanket to lessen the noise of detonations all around us. I could no longer make a distinction between my body and that of the building shaking. The window rattled as if it would burst and I saw the two silent women move away from it.

When the "all clear" signal finally sounded, I was bathed in sweat despite the freezing temperatures.

The following morning brought new anxieties and more waiting. The room was quiet, the air heavy with thoughts that found no relief in talk. After last night's air raid, a general lethargy had taken over at the approach of a new day. It takes so much energy to hope, to guard one's faith in the ultimate victory of good over evil, and not be lulled into a state of mental blackout of what the next hour may bring. The two women to my right, who had not spoken a word since I had arrived, had already cut the channels of communication that connect one human being with another and connect all of us to life. They had either exhausted all resources of human language or had lost their faith in its power to heal. They lived suspended in a universe of resignation and hopelessness. Could pain still reach them?

Breakfast was a slice of black bread with a hint of margarine and a cup of lukewarm *Ersatzkaffee*, which was of little help against the cold. It was our only diversion and we all lingered over this meager repast to give us something to do.

Some time in the afternoon, the Jewish forced laborer appeared at the door to ask me to follow him. Hope and fear rose in me. I followed him downstairs into the same vestibule where we had checked in. Two lines of children were waiting, one for boys, among them Hans, the other for girls. Hans and I exchanged smiles of recognition, caught between relief and dread. I joined the line of girls as the laborer directed me.

Somewhere to my left, the voice of a man - calm, firm, eerily warm - told us to listen quietly to his instructions. Without having seen him yet, I knew it to be the SS officer about whom I had heard so much. His measured steps moved closer to the front of the two lines until he was in view of all of us. He was indeed good looking, his features young, refined, and tinted with a confident smile. His impeccable, grey-green uniform enhanced the supple grace of his lean body. Only the death head on his cap was evidence of his sinister mission. He paced his words with deliberate smoothness.

"I am strict with the men, courteous to women, and affectionate with children." He demonstrated the latter statement by patting the dark curls of a girl in front of him. I shuddered, reminded of the talk with Miriam. His words, his face, and the death head above his forehead conveyed a contradiction too deep to comprehend. He informed us that we were allowed to go home and that we should wait for our release papers.

Standing in front of him, he told Hans and me that they had to check my father's papers more thoroughly and that he would be sent home later. I believed him, because I wanted to believe; the alternative was too unthinkable.

The first sight that met my eyes upon leaving our prison was the lone figure of a stranger standing in the entrance way to an apartment building across the street, his right hand raised in a gesture of welcome to our freedom. Farther down the street were more figures waiting for the release of those in prison, relatives or friends.

I felt connected to these people, connected by a shared anguish, a common sorrow. Yet I had no tears left when I was reunited with my mother, even tears of joy, because joy had long ago fled from our life.

As soon as we were back in our apartment, Frau Schmidt told us what had happened to Frau Philipps. The Gestapo had come to pick her up the day of our arrest. It was ghastly to see how they pushed this eighty-two-year-old woman and hardly gave her enough time to pack her few belongings.

"I felt so sorry... so ashamed at not being able to help her. They just wouldn't let me. Your Mama had gone down to be with her sister so she wouldn't have to see this. After that, we stayed up practically all night waiting for you."

She did not have to tell us what that night was like. My mother's exhausted look told us all. Even her smile at seeing us return unharmed was strained, tentative, and still worried at not seeing her husband.

My father did indeed arrive home the next day, a Sunday. We gave my mother a detailed account of the events of the last two anguished days and thought as well of the possible fate of my father's cousins, Tante Ilse and Tante Irene. Thinking of them and so many others caught in the net of the *Aktion* cast a gloom over our reunion.

Herta Gödicke came to my grandmother's store that Sunday, and related her version of the protest in Rosenstrasse. She had gone there to inquire about her mother and was told that she might be released and in the future protected from any further arrests if the daughters pledged to have her live with them. Herta agreed to it all willingly. She had heard of the demonstration and how the women faced the machine guns of the SS to demand the release of their husbands. Someone told her that at one point the fed-up women had yelled, "*Ihr Mörder*" (You murderers) to the SS pointing the machine guns at them. The SS dared not shoot, and lowered their guns.

"Can you imagine?" she asked us. "Those women broke down the walls of silence."

We looked at one another, unable to speak, but then my father turned to my mother and said, calm and proud, "And so did you, Mama. And so did you."

My good friend Steffi in 1941; she did not survive the Shoah

Chapter 5

All in a Day

So they made the people
of Israel serve with rigor,
and made their lives bitter
with hard service.
—Exodus 2:13

The start of the New Year of 1944 held out no favorable signs to Berliners. Quite the contrary. The devastation people had experienced the previous year was likely to increase with the frequency of more and more losses from air raids and defeats on the battlefield. The misery of those made homeless by the bombings was compounded by an uncommon severity of winter cold. The month of January, Berliners fretted, must have been the coldest on record. The city was held in a relentless grip of sub-zero temperatures that was taking on crisis proportions with the growing shortage of fuel. Some desperate citizens defied prohibitions by chopping down trees in the Tiergarten and other public properties or by burning pieces of furniture they could do without. Though the newspapers and radio reports still boasted of military victories, Berliners, feeling gnawing hunger and cold, knew better; their morale was low, their cynicism high.

Human life was worth no more than a dog's.

The dire losses in Leningrad and Stalingrad had turned the mood in Berlin somber, its citizens swelling with suppressed rage at the ensuing hardships and human suffering. The public outcry leveled the blame against nations hostile to Germany but, privately, some placed it where it belonged. Survivors from the Eastern Front told of momentous losses, of corpses heaped high, of horrendous sufferings and insuperable odds stacked against German soldiers, ill-prepared to cope with the Russian winter and the starvation resulting from being encircled by Russian troops.

Frau Schmidt's husband, Arnold, had been on furlough from the Russian front and he told us stories in a voice that may well have reflected the bitterness many soldiers felt at being led to the battlefield like cattle to slaughter, poorly supplied with military equipment and meager food rations. He related to us scenes of unimaginable cruelty, from bodies either being frozen or starved to death, from mutilations to cannibalism. The enemy came toward their lines like a massive human wall, he told us, multi-layered and stolid. If the first line of Russians fell, the next walked over their dead bodies until they also fell. Wave after wave... an endless resource of human sacrifices. It was worse than their guns being fired from a distance. It was psychological warfare and unnerved the German fighters until they eventually stopped firing, beaten into retreat.

And yet, the military defeats on the fronts, the disasters at home, the loss of life by the tens of thousands, only served to increase the volume of the strident voices of Hitler and Goebbels, trying to rouse the people from despair to a belief that all these deaths were sacrifices made for the greater glory of the German Reich. How many who had loved ones rotting somewhere in Russia or Africa, or under the rubble of their own homes, were consoled by that? Those we knew felt indignant at being thought foolish enough to believe this piece of propaganda spread by people who filled them with loathing. Frau Schmidt, at any rate, would turn the radio off and hiss, *"Ach, was für'n Quatsch die da reden,"* (what rubbish they are talking). My cousin Klaus had volunteered in the officers corps and was fighting somewhere in Hungary. No one knew when he would become another casualty in this beastly war.

Meanwhile at home, the nemesis from the air descended with such fury on the guilty and innocent alike that some people began to see in it a punishment for German atrocities committed against humanity. Others talked of Allied barbarity. Our friend Rudi, during a visit after a particularly heavy bombing raid, reflected aloud to us.

"Bombs, like fortune, are blind, you know. They drop their loads indiscriminately. If it's any consolation for you, these steel angels of death don't single out Jews. And as for Lady Fortuna, she is not only blind but I think she has altogether turned her back on us. We are all living near the mouth of Hell, where no birds can pass except those from the Royal Air Force."

Sitting in our shelter for hours at a time, I wanted to hear in the roar of the planes the friendly voice of someone telling me, "They are not meant for you, but for those who are against you." These imaginary voices drowned out at times the screaming of bombs and the cutting edge of fear, because they came as from a friend, a long-expected but distant friend.

After our detention and release from Rosenstrasse, my father and I had been assigned to hard labor at separate railroad stations. He was going back to Schlesischer Bahnhof to unload freight trains. I had to work at Stettiner Bahnhof, the main point of departure and arrival for troops fighting at the Eastern front.

The first time I had to go see the manager in charge of the foreign and Jewish workers, I felt like someone who had just received a death sentence.

"How old are you?" the manager asked me matter-of-factly.

"Fifteen."

"Hm," he grunted, then paused for a while before the next question. Looking closer at me, he no doubt wondered what in the world he was supposed to do with a girl like me in a place like this. If he rejects me, had been my thought, I'll be deported. But then he became business-like again.

"That's where you'll be working," was his curt announcement, pointing to the window behind him framing a railroad yard. While he was looking at my papers, my eyes had surveyed the view outside that window, showing a network of tracks with trains everywhere. I became aware of a rising wave of panic. In looking at this gigantic spider web of steel and iron in which there seemed to be no space left for anyone to walk, I was convinced that I had been saved from deportation only to end my life under the wheels of an oncoming train. As a small girl, I used to love to go on train rides, but this yard looked like a gigantic trap laid especially for me.

I made a conscious effort not to show my fear, but after hearing myself tell him, "I'll be here at a quarter to seven in the morning," my words mocked that effort; they came out as though someone were trying to strangle me. The manager, however, showed no signs of noticing anything out of the ordinary.

The terror of having seen the maze of iron found no expression at home. That night I took it to bed with me, and a dream I had uncovered the real meaning of my fear.

The tracks I had seen from the manager's office were crisscrossing my path while I stood rooted to one spot, not knowing where to turn next. On both sides of me were passenger trains full of people looking at me from their closed windows, wondering what I was going to do next. The expression on their faces was one of idle curiosity, but my temptation to ask for advice was quickly stifled when I realized that their lips were tightly pressed together, as though by an invisible clamp. The power of speech had been taken from them. Then I saw the manager coming toward me and I expected him to help me out of this iron web. But instead he was transformed into a locomotive coming straight at me. I screamed... and woke up, my hands tightly clenched, the nails digging into my palms.

My father reassured me the next day at breakfast that, of course, there was enough room for people to walk between the tracks. How else could the workers proceed with their work?

The seemingly trivial episode of disorientation when I saw the railroad tracks for the first time unnerved me for months to come. It left me with some disturbing questions. Were my fears robbing me of my reason? Or were my imaginings rather an apt reflection of the reality in which our lives were enmeshed? My dream had clearly shown me how entrapped I felt and how the indifference and silence of non-Jews only heightened that feeling. The possibility of losing my sanity before losing my life was such a frightful prospect that I turned more and more to an inner voice assuring me, "*Du bist schuldlos, du bist schuldlos*" (you are guiltless), the madness is outside, not within you."

Two sounds above all dominated my life with peremptory persistence: the shrill ringing of the alarm clock and the howling of sirens, each cutting into my sleep like the final call to judgment. The alarm woke me at five o'clock each morning and, as had become my habit, I hurled myself out of the protective warmth of my bed into the ice-cold air of the room in order to resist the temptation to stay under the covers for another luxurious five minutes. It felt like the expulsion from Eden reenacted each day, only I had ceased to find a reason for this punishment in a mindless universe. Sleep was one of the rare gifts in those days. The loss of it was felt all the more keenly as we spent countless hours in our shelter during air raids. I often envied my brother's "easy" life. Because he was not yet fourteen, he had not been called to forced labor, and was still asleep as I prepared myself for another eleven hours at Stettiner Bahnhof. What did he do with his days at home, I often wondered but never bothered to find out. We had become two separate entities; our lives no longer touched and when we did talk of our day at the end of it, we seemed to come from different countries. Only during the bombing raids did we experience the same tremors of fear for our life.

It was a cold morning in January when I pulled the covers off my bed and stood in the room fully dressed in what I had thrown on for the last air raid. We had been awakened twice during the night. The first time the sirens rang out shortly before midnight and kept us in the cellar for two and a half hours, bombs dropping in and near our district of Charlottenburg. After it was over, we went to our apartment, wide awake with the jitters that did not allow sleep to come easily. The second air raid lasted only a merciful one hour, with the distant sound of bombs dropping on a district further away.

Since I was already partly dressed, I stayed in bed for another five minutes of rest, which was hardly enough to stave off the feeling of exhaustion, yet it gave me the illusion of extra indulgence. My father was already in the kitchen preparing our breakfast of *Ersatzkaffee* and black bread with margarine.

In order to get to the kitchen, I had to tiptoe through the dining-living room where my mother lay still asleep. She had, as was her habit, stayed up long after we had gone to bed, washing and mending the dirty, torn clothes my father and I brought home from work.

My father handed me a cup of hot coffee, which we drank more for the warmth it gave than for the pleasure of its taste.

"*Guten Morgen*," I greeted him, my teeth chattering from the cold and lack of sleep. The cold entered into every corner of the apartment and every part of me like an unwelcome guest whom you cannot persuade to leave.

"Here, at least it's hot," my father said, seeing me shiver. Before the hot liquid reached my stomach, my teeth stopped chattering and I had a fleeting sense of well-being.

"How close do you think that hit was last night?" I asked my father, more to make conversation than from curiosity.

"It was close, I'm sure. Maybe a block away. Sounded like a direct hit," my father answered, rather indifferently.

"This rotten war," was all I could add to our sleepy exchange.

"Hush, *Püppchen*," my father warned me, and I knew what he was thinking, "*Die Wände haben Ohren*" (the walls have ears), an expression I'd heard my parents say ever since I was five years old. It was an expression that had then conjured up a strange picture in my mind, as I was trying to imagine what those ears in the wall might look like or where they may be hiding or, worse yet, what might happen if they heard us. Those ears had since taken on a definite image of men in brown uniforms and black boots, or wearing the button of the Party, or just any unsuspected neighbor who wanted to ingratiate himself with those in power. We had absorbed our lesson of secrecy well and knew to fear that the wrong word might come back like an arrow tinctured with poison.

Not only our speech but our very thoughts were cauterized before they could ripen into forbidden words.

After we had finished our breakfast my father informed me, almost apologetically, that there would be no cheese for lunch today. There had not been any shipment for some time, so that we had to rely on our ration cards which, for Jews, were a mockery of their very name, *Lebensmittel-karten*. A means for life? For whose life? Certainly not ours. But before we left our apartment, my father smiled and said, "Keep your fingers crossed. Maybe there will be a shipment of cheese instead of motor oil." We both opted for cheese.

Once on the street, I had to pass the building diagonally across from us at the corner of Sybelstrasse and Wilmersdorferstrasse which housed a branch of SS headquarters. It was shrouded in darkness, as on many other mornings when I left for work; the only sign of life the lone sentinel standing guard at the headquarter's side door on Sybelstrasse. My yellow star was always in full view when I passed him, but after I had gone some distance and felt myself safe under cover of the blackout, I covered it with a scarf or pocketbook "accidentally," feeling free and clean of it for a while.

The air was heavy with the acrid smell of sulfur, burnt metal, and something sweet. Was it gas... or human flesh? I remembered the detonation and shaking of our cellar last night and was suddenly afraid to come upon the site of destruction. My eyes started to sting and then I saw the remains of an apartment building a few yards away. The flames were still flickering here and there among the heap of rubble at the bottom like so many candles commemorating a departed soul. The facade was still standing, its blown-out windows looking like eyes in a skull. The air breathed silence, the silence of the grave, *Grabesstille*, was the word that came to me from a poem I once read.

I hurried past the ruin, feeling like a trespasser in the land of the dead. Life and death followed each other in such quick succession that I often felt like a sleepwalker during my waking hours.

The sky was stained blood-red with the reflections of fires burning throughout the city, consuming human lives and "monuments of human intellect." Hitler's dream of turning Berlin into the capital of the world was slowly changing it into a smoldering wasteland, a heap of ashes and broken glass. Whole sections of the city had already been leveled to the ground. I had seen piles of broken masonry and twisted steel stretching for miles from the window of the train I rode every day, and every day there were added new areas of devastation. Houses that had been only partially destroyed served as shelters for people who had escaped with their lives from burning buildings. There was no water, no electricity, no defense against the cold for these people; civilization had come to an end for them as they hid in cave-like holes.

Do they ever envy the dead?

Charlottenburg S-Bahn station was deserted at this hour in the morning. With the yellow star still covered, I boarded the train and, finding a few people seated, I uncovered it and remained standing, though there were plenty of vacant seats. Jews were forbidden to sit down, even if several places were empty.

Most of the people were asleep, wrapped in their woolen scarves and their memories of last night like frightened animals in their lairs. Fatigue marked their sallow faces, part of the greater pallor that had spread over Berlin's open wounds. What united me with these people was this forbidding grayness in the early morning hours, the stench of death everywhere after an avalanche of explosives had fallen on the city from an indifferent sky. We were fellow travelers on an endless journey through fear, but I could not travel into their inner space and put to rest the questions always present when necessity threw me into their midst: are you friend or foe? Do you want me to live or do you want me dead? All our philosophy was reduced to this simple distinction between "us" and "them," although we were all trapped on a sinking ship. The isolation I had felt so long ago on that cold day in November when I stepped on broken glass and screamed about our synagogue burning had become so embedded in me that I viewed everyone with suspicion; every stranger was linked to the persecutor. The rule of terror seemed to have overwhelmed the gentler, nobler, and compassionate impulses in our non-Jewish neighbors, because fear of reprisals had stunted them into passivity and silence. And so I had begun to divide the world into the guilty and the innocent, as weighed on the scales of justice. I saw the guilty mired down in slavish obedience to a malevolent power, while the innocent were smarting under the whip of the oppressor, waiting for the day of liberation. My cousin Klaus, in my mind, had joined the gang of mindless followers. There was no way of knowing if or when the blinders would fall from his eyes. When I looked at the people on the train with me, their sagging shoulders and worn faces, I, a forced laborer, felt freer than they, because, stripped of German citizenship, I would not have to carry the burden of German national identity and its guilt.

The smell I had noticed earlier in our neighborhood was stronger as soon as I got off the train to walk the few blocks to Stettiner Bahnhof. The pungency that stung the air told me immediately that this must have been one of the hardest hit areas of last night's attack. Perhaps Stettiner Bahnhof had gotten a direct hit. I always hoped for that, but also knew that would not change my status as a forced laborer.

One of the streets I had to pass through was cordoned off and I could see buildings either totally or partially destroyed. Low-burning fires were everywhere, the flames licking the rubble looking strangely harmless, like fires burning in a fireplace.

Further on, the scene was heartrending. People roamed the streets aimlessly, some dazed and oblivious to their surroundings. Others were sobbing hysterically. Some held on to their children's hands and the few belongings they had been able to salvage. Others were trying to get back to their homes, unable to grasp the fact that they no longer had homes, that the buildings they had lived in no longer existed or were threatened by imminent collapse. They were held back by policemen and air-raid wardens.

Bombed out! Homeless! They looked desolate.

Several rescuers were searching the rubble with kerosene lamps for possible survivors under the debris. A small girl stood holding her doll with one hand while the other pointed upward to a ruin that had been her apartment only a few hours ago. I could not see her parents anywhere.

The picture of desolation all around me blotted out all thought and words, only a hollow feeling in my stomach reminded me that there exists a pain so deep that each of us has to bear it alone. To think of this scene multiplied a hundred, a thousand times all over this ravaged land... impossible to imagine.

A policeman shook me out of my daze and ordered me to move on. I started running when I noticed that I had been clutching my bag over my yellow star as though I were holding a prayer book.

Despite the delay, I arrived at Stettiner Bahnhof on time, surprised and angry at seeing this monstrosity of steel and concrete unharmed and as solid as ever. It looked sinister and menacing with so much life around it destroyed. What a cruel irony. This gateway to the places of war and destruction still standing while the bodies of little children lay buried under tons of concrete, with no stones to mark their graves, no memorial to their senseless deaths.

Stettiner Bahnhof was a sleeping giant with a mantle of darkness covering its iron frame.

The mood of my co-workers was grim and mirrored my own inner state of shock and dismay, numbing me as much as did the icy cold. Tired faces greeted me and no one spoke much. Even our overseer's usual forceful voice was hushed to a whisper as he assigned us our tasks. There was only one person who seemed impervious to the chaos all around him, and that was our feeble-minded Gerhard, hard-working and good-natured, ignorant or indifferent to the racial boundaries set up by the state that he blithely ignored when he welcomed us with his usual, "*Guten Morgen, meine Lieben.*" The only reason he had not become a victim of the euthanasia program was because his father was a card-carrying member of the Party. The father had received a special dispensation for his son, whose job it was to pick up the litter in the railroad yard, many times going over the same area without ever complaining. He whistled while he worked, usually popular tunes he had heard on the radio, seemingly happy to be thus employed: a useful member of the Reich.

We had been assigned to the same job we did most of the time: cleaning the outside windows of trains that had come in from the Eastern front. They were coated with dust and grime accumulated over long distances and days of travel through all kinds of weather and landscapes. Each of us carried a ladder over our left shoulder and a pail with dry detergent in our right hand. There were five of us. We moved toward the train that had arrived from Russia the night before, a long train, silhouetted against the grayness of dawn. All the signs of an arduous journey through the vastness of Russia were visible on the windows, covered with so much grime that they were indistinguishable from the rest of the train, giving it the appearance of a mammoth snake that had crawled into the twentieth century from its prehistoric sleep. It was a prison on wheels, entrapping the soldiers slowly as the view of the outside world gradually disappeared through a crust of dust and ice.

Each worker had to take one car of the long train. Marcel, a foreign worker from France, Pedro from Spain, Margot, Hannah, and I, the only Jewish workers, set to work. Margot and Hannah, designated "*Geltungsjuden*" like myself, had become my friends almost immediately. I felt closer to Margot, whose quick intelligence and genial disposition appealed to me more than Hannah's rather reserved and more passive nature.

We worked fast to keep warm and to be finished with our assignment ahead of time and talk during a five or ten minute break that often sufficed to make us feel human again.

While we were still at work, a troop of female laborers from the Ukraine joined us, dust pans and brushes in hand to start the more coveted work inside the train, cleaning the floors littered with cigarette butts and miscellaneous papers left by the soldiers. They also cleaned the inside windows, and it would happen not infrequently that we would suddenly face each other through the glass without so much as a smile of acknowledgement. Even through the dirt-covered windows, the hostility between us and the Ukrainians was transparent.

There were two enviable advantages to working inside the trains, despite its back-breaking demands to bend down to sweep the floors. One, it offered shelter from the icy cold and thus protection from frostbite. Two, there was always an abundance of cigarette butts, items that quickly disappeared from the floor into the ample pockets of the Ukrainians wearing bulky shirts and jackets. They looked like reapers during the grape harvest, with their backs bent over their loot, their kerchiefs pulled over their foreheads, vying with each other for the larger remnants of stale cigarettes.

The grime on the windows was particularly stubborn during the winter months when the trains sped through icy winds that froze the soot and dust onto the glass. Our faces too were soon covered with a fine layer of soot mixed with the powdery detergent we used for scrubbing off the dirt. On the first day of work we had looked at each other and broken into laughter, until we discovered that we had been looking at a mirror image of ourselves. "*Schornsteinfeger*" (chimney sweeps) was the name we gave our little group of window cleaners from that day on.

One day before we were given our assignments, I noticed an unusually dark and closed expression on Marcel's usually jovial and open face, while Margot, who had the most cheerful disposition of us all, seemed especially pained and withdrawn. I was therefore not surprised when she whispered to us hurriedly, "I need to talk to you... later."

On our way to the station, we burst into talk, saving, however, the more important news for our lunch break.

"Let's hurry," I encouraged the others to walk faster, "so we can beat the Ukrainians."

They all understood that I was hoping to collect some cigarette butts for my mother who would occasionally smoke when pressures mounted, defying doctors' orders to give up cigarettes altogether.

"No such luck with these harpies," Margot commented.

"And they don't even smoke," Hannah remarked, puzzled. "What do they do with all that loot?"

Marcel shot her a look of surprise and then enlightened her. "They sell the stuff on the black market in exchange for food. Haven't you ever heard about that? We use it too - that is, when we have something to exchange."

Yes, we had heard of black market activities, but they were inaccessible to Jews. If caught, Jews were subject to deportation immediately.

For some time we had noticed that our foreman consistently gave the indoor jobs to our Ukrainian co-workers, and we concluded that he must have become a partner in their illicit deals, perhaps for a small amount of butter, meat, or coffee in return for his favoritism.

"You know the saying," Margot said, "one hand washes the other."

We had meanwhile come to the assigned track and, sure enough, there they were... our gray sisters of the labor force, waiting on the platform with their tools, ready to disgorge the serpent from the East after it had spilled its load of tired and bedraggled occupants.

These women, in their heavy gray dresses and scarves wound around their heads, their faces telling of the roughness of peasant life that dries the skin and deadens the soul, were a pathetic sight. They had been dragged from their native soil to this foreign land against their will, forced, like us, to do slave labor for their conquerors, yet always willing to fawn upon the men in charge of them and looking down on those just a rung or two below them - us, the Jews who, like them, were considered vermin by the 'master race.' I might have pitied them, had it not been for their virulent, unabashed anti-Semitism by which they tried to align themselves with our persecutors who had pillaged their land, raped their women, and killed their men and children. What a dour-looking bunch they were, waiting on the platform, wrapped in their shapeless clothes and their ancient hatred of us, begrudging us a few miserable cigarette butts thrown away by the men of the 'victorious' German army.

I could not hate them, no, but I will never forget their pitiful rivalry with us, the entrenched fear and fanatical hostility towards Jews that ran through their history like a black ribbon.

We watched the soldiers tottering out of the train from Russia with heavy bags slung over their stooped shoulders. We waited until they had left and there was enough room for us to start cleaning the windows, crusted over as usual with frozen soot.

Having worked there for several months, we had become quite adept at gauging the progress of the war merely by watching the soldiers' expressions and movements as they filed out of their compartments. Though fatigued from the long journey, their eyes and mouths told of a different fatigue. Looking at them was like looking at a steadily falling barometer, as a defeat for the Third Reich became ever more likely and everyone knew that the advertised victories of the German army was a dream dreamed only by fools. These soldiers knew that they were fighting a losing war and we could see it in the haunted look in their eyes, their drooping shoulders and slackened step.

Their exhaustion and hopelessness added to our own and if I had been free to speak with them I would have told them, "We are all cogs in a system gone berserk." Most looked past us, but a few actually extended verbal greetings as if the yellow star guaranteed some kind of solidarity between us. Perhaps they had seen what was being done to Jews in the East, perhaps they had witnessed mass executions and mass graves, perhaps some had felt helpless and hated what they had seen. It never happened, at any rate, that any one of them directed a harsh or derogatory remark at us. Rather the opposite was true. There was one of them in particular who told us in strong Berlin dialect, "Just leave them windows dirty. There ain't nothin' to see outta' there anyhow."

Watching them get off the train was like seeing ourselves when no one was looking. They looked so tired, so hopelessly tired, their eyes full of the deaths and extremes of human suffering they had seen. There was death everywhere: in this city, in the cities of Europe, in the vast cold steppes of Russia, in the hot clime of Africa. The earth was again soaked with the blood of Abel. Many of the returning soldiers admitted that they had experienced more fear sitting in a bomb shelter waiting for the bombs to hit than on the battlefield where they could confront the enemy gunfire with weapons of defense.

We set to work on the train while it was still in the station. It did not take long before it was ready for another feeding into the jaws of death. The windows were once again impeccably clean, until cold and dust would form a crust on them to entomb those inside.

Time for lunch was a special time, a time when verbal nourishment became a momentary substitute for actual food; for thirty minutes our humanity was restored to us and we were able to speak from the heart. The province of language was ours again and we laid siege to it like a pack of hungry wolves.

Lunch, as a rule, consisted of a steady diet of black bread and margarine or a cold potato or, if lucky, I might provide a piece of cheese. In time, it earned me the nickname, "*Käse-Rita*," and my contribution to our lunches was received like manna from heaven.

As everyone was unpacking their meager lunches, I had to tell them that there had not been a shipment of cheese for some time, but that a turn for the better was expected soon.

Pedro had gone to join some friends and the four of us, Marcel, Margot, Hannah, and I found a car in one of the trains and, as we so often did, had our lunch and some privacy for talk there. Though there was no one within hearing distance, we always kept our voices low and our ears pricked for possible intruders.

Marcel, who had been noticeably withdrawn from the very beginning of that day, opened the conversation, speaking in his broken German, his voice choked with emotion and barely audible.

Marcel was living in one of the barracks set up near the station for housing foreign laborers and, coming straight to the point, he told us that bombs, obviously meant for the railroad station had hit two of the barracks. Marcel was living in barrack Number 3 and, when they heard the familiar sound of bombs falling, someone in the room had just enough time to yell, "under the beds," when the first bomb hit, then another and another. Marcel felt sure that they were going to be next, but the planes went off to another target. Every window in their barrack was shattered. He had counted three bombs, but when he went outside after the all-clear signal, he stood aghast at the devastation that met his eyes. Dazed by the sight, he could not move at first, but, soon recovering, ran as fast as his legs would carry him to barrack Number 7 where his best friends were housed. He knocked against other survivors who were just as shaken and confused and were all looking for friends or beginning rescue work. The place was absolute mayhem, everyone in their night clothes, stumbling over fallen debris, and coughing from inhaling so much smoke.

When he came to Number 7, he refused to believe what he saw and thought he must have gone in the wrong direction in all the confusion. Barrack 8 had received a direct hit, it was a heap of smoldering ashes and broken bodies, some burned beyond recognition. There was no need for rescuers. Part of Barrack 7 had collapsed from being hit, the other half had remained standing, except there were no survivors. He saw his friends, a young married couple, still in their bed... naked... with no injuries to their bodies... their arms around each other as if asleep. They looked so peaceful, altogether at odds in their last embrace of love with the violent destruction and death all around that he had difficulty believing they were no longer alive. When he had to accept the fact, he went to help bury the dead, all those mangled and charred bodies recovered from underneath the twisted metal. No one got any more sleep that night.

"But what I will remember for the rest of my life is the picture of perfect love in the midst of so much hatred," Marcel ended in a voice choked with tears.

We were silent.

The paucity of language can be compensated best by the knowledge that the scene Marcel had just described can have its proper receptacle only in the stillness of the heart. I too wanted to rescue the image of love from the carnage of war, but could not reconcile it with the repugnance I felt at such unholy wastefulness. Death had already claimed so many innocents. How much longer before the voracious appetite for victims would be stilled in those that feed on the lives of others, worse than vultures, who will touch only carrion?

We had time left in our lunch break and I remembered Margot's hurried whisper earlier that she had something important to tell us. Looking at her to remind her of that, I saw the pained expression deepening in her face after Marcel had finished his account, her head bent down, her eyes looking at her hands clasped between her knees, a characteristic pose of hers when she was deep in thought. Margot and her twin brother worked for an underground Zionist organization helping Jews go into hiding or escape to Palestine. She was honor-bound not to tell us about it except for some occasional allusion to the success of their activities. Here was one such occasion.

A man had come to the organization with the most harrowing account of his detention and eventual escape from a concentration camp where he had witnessed countless atrocities. One of them involved him personally. Some SS guards were looking for a diversion from their routine duties and had apparently decided on having a sharp shooting contest, only instead of using the customary targets for such practices, one of them had the idea of using human heads... Jewish heads. They chose several of the Jewish inmates and marched them to a lake nearby. What was noteworthy in their choice of inmates was that they had to be related to another inmate, whether as wife, husband, brother, sister, cousin, aunt, or uncle. They forced some to enter the lake until the water reached their necks. The family members of those in the lake were forced to watch how the heads above the water became the targets for the SS, who cheered and laughed whenever one of them had succeeded and the unfortunate victim went to his watery grave. If any of those on the shore watching their loved ones sink below the water looked away or covered their eyes, they were ordered to enter the lake and suffer the same fate. A few went voluntarily to join a brother or sister, husband or wife. This man's own cousin was among those forced to stand in the water. By the time he realized what was happening, he only saw the terror in his cousin's eyes and it momentarily paralyzed him into complete non-comprehension. The whole scene began to seem unreal to him. It was as though he had stepped out of his body, saw himself leaving the shore and walking toward the electric fence of the camp to end it all. "Who wants to remain among the living after having seen such bestiality?" he had asked his listeners. But then a sudden surge of life swept through him, and only one thought made him want to cling to life, 'I must live in order to tell my survival story to the world, and bear witness to the inhuman crimes committed by a legitimate government.' When the ordeal was finally over and his life had been spared, he looked at the surface of the lake. It was calm and neutral, hiding its terrible secret. Sunlight was reflected on the surface of the water, making it sparkle as if studded with so many diamonds, his cousin one of them. He took a long look at his tormentors, inscribing every detail of their features in his memory, and planned his daring escape.

"He wants to survive, whatever risks may be involved," Margot concluded her account, "obsessed with the idea of finding the perpetrators some day to hand them over to a court of justice, thus avenging the death of his cousin and many other innocent victims."

Despite being hungry, it seemed preposterous to think of eating after having heard Margot's account. Food was a celebration, an affirmation of life, and we had been banished to the land of the dead, with the taste of dust in our mouths. What felt like burning coals inside me found release in a thought I spoke out loud, "And to think of this incident repeated a hundred, a thousand times over and over again in the death traps of Europe..."

Tears brought some temporary relief before we had to go back to work, and we offered them as a final farewell, a last prayer for the dead.

———

The cold always increased as the sun was beginning to sink below the horizon. We performed our tasks like automatons, our hands, feet, and thoughts frozen. I wanted to find a hiding place to be alone with my rage, but there was none, only the open railroad yard, swept by cold winds and the cold eyes of our indifferent German co-workers.

Late in the afternoon, our foreman, a kindly German in his forties, assigns us the job we all dread the most. It is a nightmare for me, recalling the ride in the stroller going through the tunnel. We have to go down into ditches, six feet deep and the width of two tracks above, to oil certain joints under the railroad cars. Some of these joints are placed right next to the car's lavatory, and the revulsion I experienced the first time I had to do it overwhelms me again. The stench around the area of the toilets is vile, even on the coldest days; in the summer it is insufferable. I struggle against wanting to shout a loud, clear "NO" at our foreman every time he assigns us to go down there, with the train stretching ahead to what seems like miles in all its hideous blackness, dripping oil and excrement from its obscene belly. The kerchief I wear at all times is flimsy protection against this miasma from hell.

We carry cans full of thick black oil that brush against the legs of our pants until the oil soaks down to the skin. The dark stain it leaves for days is the mate to our yellow star. As hard as I try to keep the can from my body, the effort it takes is too tiring and often makes me careless; my poor mother is then saddled with getting the pants clean again while I try to get the stain off my leg with an abrasive cleansing powder that chafes my skin. It is a losing battle.

Just as we come to the end of the train and have finished oiling the last cars, my worst nightmare is enacted.

Hannah and I are on our way out of the ditch to join the others when we see a locomotive approaching, barring our access to the steps leading out of the ditch. We stand completely still, at a loss what to do. Just then our foreman comes running ahead of the locomotive, waving his arms to warn us not to move. As soon as he is within shouting distance, he yells.

"Kneel all the way down and put your hands over your heads so the hot steam water won't drip on you."

There is just enough time to follow his instructions as we hear the locomotive rumble overhead. Pressed against the side of the ditch, I bend my head between my knees. I hold my breath. It is over before I start to exhale, and the silence that follows the roar of the locomotive is deep as sleep. Still shaking in every limb, we run to the steps where our foreman greets us with a smile of relief, "You gave me a good scare. Good thing I was near."

The last two hours before work ends are always the hardest. We had come to the end of our strength to perform the assigned tasks and to endure the cold after sunset. It was that time of day when the thought of going home to thaw out my frozen hands and feet in the relative warmth of our living room felt like someone holding a life net for you.

The railroad yard was all in darkness; only the dim light from lamp posts and the sparse glow from our kerosene lamps pierced the black curtain that protected the city from enemy eyes. The heavens also had withdrawn their lights, as if they could not bear to look upon the mutilation of their companion earth. Looking at the darkened sky, I often asked myself whether God too had turned away from the madness of human affairs, leaving it up to us to disentangle the deadly net wherein one human being entraps another.

We had to grope our way through the maze of tracks running across the yard, a reminder of my earlier fantasies of getting caught in their intricate labyrinth. That fear had vanished with the growing familiarity with the yard. The darkness was beginning to feel more like a veil covering the tedious reality of tracks and trains, tracks and trains.

Because it was too hazardous to work outside after dark on our ladders with barely a light guiding our movements, our foreman had assigned us to clean the inside windows of a train being readied to go East at the break of day, a task usually reserved for our Ukrainian co-workers.

We welcomed the chance to get out of the cold wind and dank night air. The Ukrainians were nowhere in sight, and thus we had no rivals for this rare luxury. What made it even more auspicious for me was the fact that our foreman had paired us off to work on alternate cars: Margot and I in one, Hannah and Marcel in another, until we had come to the end of a train long enough to keep us busy for the remainder of the working time. I was glad for the chance to be alone with Margot for a while without Hannah clinging to her like a shadow. A conversation with Margot always proved fertile ground for the growth of new ideas or exploration of deeper feelings, in contrast to talking with Hannah, who was more of a listener than an initiator of dialogue.

As soon as Margot and I had made sure that we were alone and unobserved, our words rushed out at first and then vanished in an inarticulate muddle, so great was our need to break through the silence that had followed the stories told during lunch time, when our pain, our rage, and our fears lay submerged in us.

There was one item of news I had not told anyone yet, and I saw an opportunity while working alone with Margot. She had always been a sympathetic and eager listener to my tales about my friendship with Mira, and I knew I could elicit the right response from her.

"I received word about Mira the other day. A young man, close to our age and also a 'Geltungsjude' like us, had been interned in Grosse Hamburgerstrasse during the week-long round-up in February and March. He had been there for a whole week because there had not been enough space in Rosenstrasse. There he learned the story of Mira that had spread throughout the detention center. Mira had gone through nearly eighty seizures in the week that she and her parents were detained there."

"That's almost ten a day..." Margot could not finish her thought. We both knew that the chances of Mira surviving even the transport to whatever camp she was destined to go to were slim. After a while, not surprisingly, we spoke of God.

We began our talk with the conviction that God had nothing to do with the events that were unfolding day by day, that God had simply stepped out of history and placed the responsibility for the horrors committed on the shoulders of the entire human race. And yet, we could not avoid the torturous questions: why, if there was a God, was He letting it all happen? Why did He not thunder from the clouds to punish the guilty by sending the ten plagues again?

Margot then related a memorable lesson one of her teachers of Jewish history had once taught the class, which had guided her actions ever since. The history of the first Hebrews, he had told them, has been evolving. The centuries of the Bible beginning with Moses up to the age of the prophets, when God manifested Himself in admonishments to the children of Israel, is the state of childhood. The state of adulthood begins with the fall of the second Temple, initiating the age of the Rabbis and the writing of the Talmud when the word of God became more accessible to human scrutiny, interpretation, and application to human conduct in a changing world. The Talmud liberated Jews from blind obedience to dogma to interpret biblical passages and laws in accordance with human needs and with the flux of history. The one immutable guide to human conduct outside the Ten Commandments, the same teacher maintained, is to love your neighbor as yourself. A disregard for this simple axiom had been the cause of innumerable persecutions of Jews and of wars among nations all through history. Perhaps, her teacher had concluded, the human race is still in a state of childhood, for love among adults requires patience, compassion, and the rule of reason.

What Margot said made sense to me, and when I asked her whether she had retained her faith in God, she shrugged her shoulders and said simply, "I don't know, but I often fear my faith got smothered in the ashes of our synagogues." She went on to speak with such certainty of things closest to her heart that I began to see the real Margot for the first time. In speaking of our possible survival, she claimed that we have a sacred obligation to make sure that what is happening to Jews under Hitler should never happen again. We must not rely on God for the future survival of the Jewish people but must rely on ourselves. When I asked her how that might come about, she plunged into her favorite topic with such fervor it seemed that everything she had ever told us about it before had merely been a preamble to the one idea that had helped sustain her through all the difficult times: her dream of *Eretz* Israel, the land of Israel. It was the land of our forefathers, of Abraham and Isaac, of King David and King Solomon, where her dream of a Jewish state would fulfill itself.

While we were scrubbing the dirt off the windows for German soldiers ready to fight against our liberators, Margot stepped out of time and became rhapsodic when she projected herself onto the soil of Palestine. There she would perform any menial task required of her; there she would slave with love to build houses where the wind had played with open spaces; there she would work under the desert sun in search of hidden wells; there she would help change the barren sand into fertile soil to nurture future citizens; there they would all live peacefully side by side with their Arab neighbors, their ancient cousins and, if that were not possible, she was ready to fight them. It was in the land of the ancient Israelites that Margot envisioned our true victory over Hitler.

Margot's zeal was enviable; I felt impoverished because there was no such utopia beckoning me into the future and, should I survive, I felt no such mission to justify my survival. Margot had never spoken to me so openly, so sincerely, with such desperate and ardent urgency of her belief in a return to *Eretz* Israel. Any doubts I may have had of her merely mimicking Zionist rhetoric were quickly replaced by a new understanding of what constituted the source of her geniality, her vivacity and positive spirit in the darkest of times.

Time had passed quickly while we talked and, to our surprise, we had come to the end of the train where Hannah and Marcel were waiting for us. A few minutes were left before it was time to go home at six o'clock. We chose a first-class compartment to sit in, luxuriating on the dark red velvet covered seats that had been occupied earlier by high ranking officers of the German *Wehrmacht*. We chuckled at this ironic reversal of our positions and snubbed our noses at the whole gang of madmen. We agreed that we were all far too tired and too full of the day's news to do much talking. We would rather forget that an endless string of days would follow with no change in sight. Marcel yawned noisily as soon as he hit the soft upholstery and we each yawned in response. That started our little experiment to prove that yawns were contagious. We laughed between yawns and, when our eyes were moist with tears, we knew they were tears of pleasure and not of pain. The tension of another hard day had been somewhat relieved. When we finally said good-bye we felt assured of our friendship.

The ride home on the elevated train always seemed endless after a long day of work; the need for rest, a change of clothes, a hot meal, even if it was only cabbage soup, was tantamount to physical pain.

It was still early evening when I stepped off the train in eager anticipation of being home. There were no street lamps to light my way through total darkness, but having walked the same route so many times, I was familiar with every turn and bump on the road and, like a blind person, felt more than saw my way home.

I had gone only a few yards from Charlottenburg station when the sound of sirens screamed through the streets. I started to run, hoping to reach our street before the planes arrived. Suddenly something obstructed my way and I fell upon what seemed like a solid object, but what I later discovered to have been a huge pile of broken glass. The roar of planes could already be heard in the distance. Driven by fear, I ran faster, vaguely aware of something wet running down my left leg into my shoe. The bombs started falling nearby just as I reached our shelter. My family was relieved to see me. When I showed them my knee, I was shocked to see a deep cut, triangular in shape and bleeding profusely. Our neighbors from below, Dr. and Frau Kaiser, prepared the First-Aid kit, examined the wound to make sure there were no splinters left, then cleaned and bandaged it. "A small scar is all you will have as a souvenir of this night," Dr. Kaiser said prophetically.

Fortunately the air raid was of short duration and no bombs had fallen in our vicinity. We were sure that some planes had lost their way to another city and had dropped some of their load on Berlin just for fun, *aus Spass*, lest we forget them.

Upstairs in the apartment, my mother heated up the barley soup she had prepared for our evening meal and, though eating it reluctantly on other days, I welcomed it as though it were Crème de Vichyssoise. While we were eating our soup and a plain piece of black bread, my father suddenly raised his hand and shouted, "*Halt.*" He went to get his coat and fished out something that had a very familiar smell to it. "*Butterkäse,*" we all cried in unison, and I could not help but add, "So, it's cheese instead of motor oil," to which my mother gave me a puzzled look. My father and I exchanged knowing glances at this allusion to our morning conversation. We all settled back in our chairs and my father assumed his characteristic pose that said let me tell you a story. And he did.

A large trainload of cheese had at last arrived and everyone helped themselves to generous portions after a long dearth of food deliveries. My father filled his pockets full of this precious commodity, passed inspection without incident, and hoped the cold weather would keep the cheese from melting. But the train he boarded was filled to capacity with people pushing and shoving each other, with the result that the compartment was slowly generating its own heat from so many bodies in motion, a situation my father dreaded. He felt as though he were in a sauna. Before too long, he noticed a strong odor quite close to him, rather pungent and slightly sour. At first he attributed it to the many people going home from work and paid it no more attention. Someone hasn't washed for a while, he thought to himself, until he noticed, much to his consternation, that the smell emanated from him; from the pockets of his coat. He felt embarrassed, but then the realization that the cheese was melting next to his overheated body threw him into a panic. *Herrgott!* he thought, what if someone discovered the smell was coming from him and that it was cheese. How did a Jew come by cheese? His immediate impulse was to get off at the next station, but he changed his mind - he could not possibly walk home, however safe it might be. People around him were starting to look at him directly, which made him sweat even more from fright. They backed away, crowding each other more than was necessary. Quite a few people got off, others moved further away from him. Soon there was so much space created around him that his body temperature dropped down to normal and he could relax somewhat for the rest of the ride.

"What I thought interesting," he finished his story, "is that until they smelled the cheese, no one seemed to mind standing next to a Jew, especially next to a smelly Jew, some perhaps thinking of me as the stereo-typical *Stinkjude*; tonight I couldn't even blame them."

My mother divided the cheese as usual but with an added air of rever-ence, giving my father the larger share in recognition of his having passed this trial by fire unscathed, though with knees shaking long afterwards.

Soon after supper, the electricity was turned off for the remainder of the night. The stump of a candle was our only source of light until it was time for bed. Even candles were rationed.

I felt tired in body and in spirit. The calm of the room, the flicker from the candle dancing here and there amidst the various pieces of my mother's crystal, like so many stars coming out in the night sky, soon in-duced a welcome drowsiness and I felt emptied of all thought. I relished this moment of family unity as though it might last forever.

My father's story had stirred a memory in me of my one and only at-tempt at stealing. I was close to four years old and the proud owner of a beautiful baby doll which looked so life-like to me that I lavished all the attention and affection on it that one would give to a real baby. That was precisely how I thought of her, a real person with real needs. It happened one day while my mother and I were shopping in a large and busy depart-ment store called "Wertheim," that we came across a counter filled with accessories for dolls. I urged my mother to stop and look at this tempting display. Amidst the articles of dresses, sweaters, caps and coats, there was a case full of small jewelry for dolls. My eyes lighted on an object I did not think could exist in such minuscule version. It was a small gold ring with a tiny red stone that held my sole attention. I knew it would fit my doll perfectly; the thought soon metamorphosed into an act. My eyes stayed glued on it until I could almost hear it whisper to me, "Take me home! Take me!" My hand obeyed this call. Before I knew it, the tiny object was clasped tight between my fingers and disappeared into one of my coat pockets. No one had noticed it, I marveled.

When my mother and I finally left the store, I still could not believe I had escaped detection, eager to reach the safety of home.

I did not fully claim ownership of the theft until I put the ring on my doll's finger. The ring was a perfect fit, except it altered her baby nature rather jarringly. That discovery brought with it a disturbing thought. Even if I should succeed in hiding this ring from the view of my immediate family, there was someone from whom my secret could not be hidden. *Der liebe Gott* had seen it all and I was sure to incur his censure for having violated the eighth commandment if I continued to gloat over it and enjoy the fruit of my wrongdoing. Under cover of night, I pulled the ring off the doll's finger, opened the bedroom window and threw it down into the backyard where I knew several bushes were growing. God will find it there, I reasoned, sure that someone was watching, not in anger, but in loving forbearance. It had looked out of place on the baby doll anyway.

That night, as I remembered my own attempt at stealing, the calm continued with no air raid breaking it.

Chapter 6

Underground

Our days on the earth are
like a shadow, and there is
no abiding.
—1 Chronicles 29:15

"Roosevelt *ist tot*." I had just heard the announcement of his death on my aunt's radio on April 12, 1945. I rushed home to tell my family, shaken by the news but even more so by what followed; Hitler had gloated afterwards, "The final victory is near at hand, now that the warmonger Roosevelt is dead."

The death of Roosevelt momentarily injected new life into the ebbing strength of the *Wehrmacht*, its soldiers eager all of a sudden to risk their lives for the vision of victory the Fuhrer dangled before them as bait. Dying for the *Vaterland* seemed a better alternative than meeting the wrath of the conquerors.

But it was a dismal day for us. The death of Roosevelt flung our hope for a second Moses into utter darkness.

As soon as my father came home from work, we deluged him with questions about this man Truman, only a name to us, who was going to succeed Roosevelt. We wanted to know, as though my father were privy to state secrets, whether this new president would be friend or foe to Jews.

"Even though Roosevelt could have done more for Jews trapped in Europe by extending the quotas for emigration," my father replied, "he did open the doors to many, as you well know from my work in the emigration department. The question is will Truman do the same for anyone who may survive this war and wants to leave Germany, the land stained with our blood."

My mother, undaunted in her optimism and faith in enough good left in the world, responded with confidence in her voice.

"I believe he will be like Roosevelt, perhaps even more so once the truth of the Nazi menace will emerge. The whole world will grieve with us. We will have friends, you'll see."

"Let's hope so," my father said, and blew out the candle as a sign that it was time to get some sleep before we would waken to more uncertainties.

The city of Berlin was moribund. The main arteries of transportation that supplied it with vital necessities were clogged with rubble left by the Allied bombings. The trainloads of cheese my father unloaded were becoming a rare commodity. Whenever there was a shipment, only a morsel would reach our table because inspections of the workers became stricter and more punitive. My mother's ingenuity in producing meals had all but exhausted itself in her continual battle with the diminishing supplies. During the winter months we often had to be thankful that we had as much as frozen potatoes or turnips to eat despite their ghastly sweet taste.

Life was experienced as a dull and constant ache. Every conversation ended with the same refrain, "How much longer can it last?" "Who will be here first? Russians or Americans?" It no longer mattered to our family who would rescue the dying city, though it mattered to most Germans. They were of one accord in anticipating retribution from their Russian conquerors.

Hitler would not surrender, the daily bulletins announced. Berlin had become his fortress that had to be defended to the last man. The young and the old, the able-bodied and the feeble alike became the new warriors on the front line Berlin had become. We all felt that this was Hitler's final hour and that he would drag the whole city with him rather than deliver it into the hands of his enemies. Rumors that Hitler had gone mad consolidated into fact. Even some Nazis felt trapped in this snake pit. My father's solemn prediction that Germany's darkest hour would herald a new beginning for us was soothing balm for our frayed nerves.

Like waves crashing on the shore, rumors of the advancing Red Army reached us finally and ended our suspense. People dreaded its coming like the visitation of the ten plagues upon the Egyptians, an appropriate parallel. The bombs dropped from British and American aircraft had been anonymous, they had no human face or voice. But the Russians, the Russians had features like us, anger like us; they could look us in the eye, see us wince with fright or defiance, and they could use us as objects for their vengeance.

"They will come like the Erinyes in an ancient tragedy to avenge the murder of their loved ones. They will exact punishment, to do unto the Germans what Germans have done unto them. But they will spare you," Onkel Rudi declared in a near oracular tone. We wanted to believe him, but rumors of Russian atrocities already committed in other parts of Germany trickled in and shook our faith in their ability to make distinctions between the guilty and the innocent once furor and vodka asserted their mastery. No one expected justice from the victorious Red Army. Deportations to Siberia were spoken of in the same breath as the rape of women.

Fear was contagious. I was not immune to it. I put no trust in the reassurances that the Russians would do no harm to Jewish women, remembering my history lessons about pogroms in Russia, long before Hitler. And I remembered my Ukrainian co-workers and their spiteful anti-Semitism; I wondered how many like them might be among the conquering troops, our liberators. And so I joined in the general paranoia and tried not to think of the worst scenario.

On the morning of April 20, 1945, another kind of paranoia held Berliners fast in its grip. They felt sure that Allied bombers would want to give

Hitler a birthday present with a clear message that this would be his last. The Thousand Year Reich was crumbling into dust and ashes; the dream of a megalomaniac was dissipating along with the smoke that enveloped the city like an unwanted lover.

The rumbling malcontent of the restless and disgruntled population threatened an eruption. To ease the tension Goebbels issued a special ration of food per person: one pound of meat, half a pound of rice and legumes each, one pound of sugar, some malt coffee, some real coffee, and a jar of preserves. Frau Schmidt and Lydia, who had been moved into Frau Phillips' empty apartment (some said in return for favors sold to Gestapo men) cynically referred to these "gifts" as "*Himmelfahrtsrationen*," rations for a trip to heaven, as there was barely enough water or gas for cooking these items. While they were being distributed, the distant drone of guns added an even more sinister tone to these hollow appeasements. "It's like the last meal given to criminals before their execution," Frau Schmidt commented, half in jest and half in bitterness.

It was true. The Russians had reached the outskirts of Berlin from where they pelted the city with artillery fire in preparation to take it street by street, house by house, stone by stone. The sky at night was aglow with blood-red reflections of the burning city. The thunder of distant guns echoed like ancestral drums, indistinguishable at first. But as the Russian army advanced, the staccato frequency of the guns cut the air like a giant whip.

My family waited for the unknown with a mixture of anxiety and excitement. We could not yet fathom the downfall of the Third Reich until we could see Soviet tanks rolling down our streets and I could greet the First Russian soldier with, "*Ya yevreika*," I am Jewish, a bit of the vocabulary I had picked up from my Ukrainian co-workers. Would the soldiers respect it?

Not long after, we were astonished to see that a barricade, stretching from our house to the house across the street, had been erected overnight.

Berlin, now the front line in the war, was taking steps to ward off or at least delay the advance of Russian tanks. Most of the food stores were located on the other side of the barricade and it became thus a daily challenge to climb over it in order to get even a loaf of bread.

Another surprise was announced by Lydia.

"Did you know," she said, entering our living room with a big grin, "that the SS housed across the street have gone... left... fled...before the Russians could get to them? One of them told me some time ago they were planning their escape routes way ahead of time, that they would leave no trace behind them, and hide in countries offering them asylum. Those cowards also have fat Swiss bank accounts. *Na ja*... good riddance."

Meanwhile, the shelling from Russian artillery pounded the city without pause day and night. One sound above all others, unfamiliar to our ears with its frightening and prolonged screeching, had a particularly ominous whine. We remembered that Herr Schmidt had once told of hearing it at the Eastern front. The Russians called them "*Katushkas,*" and the Germans renamed them "*Stalinorgel,*" a sardonic allusion to their highly destructive power, tearing everything they hit into shreds.

Our air-raid warden called an emergency meeting to discuss the next steps to be taken for the building's protection. My father, the Jew, was included in this gathering and, because of the sudden change of events, became one of its main members. Things were indeed changing with the speed of lightning. The participants of this meeting reached an agreement that all the tenants should move to the basement for shelter for the duration of the siege. The date to do so was set for April 24. Berliners in other parts of the city had already begun their underground existence.

We moved our clothes and whatever food we had left to our small room in the cellar, still separated from the larger room by order of Frau Burger, a Gestapo woman who had recently moved in to our building. Everyone but our family was staying in the common air-raid shelter, including Frau Burger, with her daughter Felizitas. Meals were to be cooked outside the entrance to our shelter on a kerosene stove, a risky business in the first few days of steady bombardments. If there was any sense of romantic adventure to our new life, it was that most of our activities were performed under the soft light of candles, masking thus the gloomy aspect of our shrunken world.

Our air-raid warden advised us to fill our tubs with water in case it was needed for extinguishing fires and, of course, for cooking and drinking after some of the water had been boiled.

We crawled like moles into our hiding places to begin our life below for an indeterminate length of time. Our yellow stars were packed away, ready to be used again if circumstances should call for it.

So there we were, huddled together in a place that allowed little movement during the day and even less space for sleeping at night when we went into fetal positions. Perched together like this, breathing the same musty air, using the one toilet, exchanging whatever scant information could still reach us, we were encircled by a few meters of damp walls that served as our protection from the random shelling. There was, of course, no longer any use for sirens. Artillery shells fell unpredictably. Berlin had become another Leningrad, only the names of the victims had been exchanged.

Cut off from the outside world, we lived entombed like that for four days. After the fourth day, the frequency of the attacks changed in our favor. The intervals between bombings grew longer and more predictable. They offered some chance for brief shopping trips and cooking time. We learned to measure the advance of the troops by the sound of their artillery and hoped that our district of Charlottenburg would be spared the final battle, hoping that the barricade would not become a battleground for German and Russian soldiers.

On the fifth day something unexpected happened. Frau Burger appeared at the door of our shelter and asked permission to join us with her daughter. We did not dare to refuse her admittance because we were still not sure what turn events might take. We understood her motives; as Jewish victims of the Nazi regime, surely the Russians would not punish us. Now, in the zero hour, she wanted to prove her allegiance with the very family she had ousted from the common air-raid shelter with "*Juden raus!*"

How vulnerable this member of the invincible master race had suddenly become, and how craven for the protection of our yellow star.

Her daughter Felizitas and I had become friends in the short time we had been confined to these dank quarters. Our connection deepened and jumped the artificial barriers set up by the racial laws of the state. She herself had remained remarkably immune to the propaganda of hate and vilification of the Jews in her midst and had not succumbed to the ideology her mother espoused. Felizitas, at fifteen, had a refreshingly childlike innocence, accented by a gentle demeanor in speech and manner toward everyone. Her nickname "Fee" (elf) suited her well. Both in appearance and disposition she was like a good fairy in a land full of demons, in contrast to her mother who was working for the powers of darkness. It seemed all the good resided in the daughter, which in the mother lay crusted over with the practices of a corrupt regime. This regime was coming to an end just in time to save one young person from becoming enmeshed in it.

Now that we are in the sixth day of the siege, our supply of water is running so low that my father decides to go upstairs to draw from our reserves. Hans and I volunteer to go with him. While we are standing in our living room, we hear the familiar howl of a *Stalinorgel* coming closer so quickly that my father has barely time to shout, "Away from the windows... into the hall." As soon as we reach the hall, we hear a deafening explosion that throws us against the wall. I am trembling so much that I can hardly tell whether it is me or the house shaking. A breathless silence ensues while we wait for another hit.

"That was awfully close," my father mumbles. "I wonder where it fell." We wait a while longer until we think it is safe to leave. We fill our containers with water and hurry downstairs to the cellar where everyone sits paralyzed with shock. My mother is ashen-faced but smiles with relief as soon as she sees us. An unspoken thought permeates the stillness around us: did we escape the Nazi prowler for twelve years only to be caught by a katushka before our liberation?

My mother finally asks the question that was on all our minds. "Do you think it hit near the store?"

The cessation of artillery fire continues. When we feel sure that it is another respite from the shelling, my father asks me to go to the bakery around the corner to get some bread. "I think it will be safe for another twenty minutes," he reassures me, familiar with the pattern by now, and so I prepare to leave.

As soon as I reach the street, my first task in the outside world since our going underground is to scale the barricade to get to the bakery on Wilmersdorferstrasse that runs perpendicular to our street. Once I am at the corner of Sybelstrasse and Wilmersdorferstrasse, I stop in amazement. Is this the same neighborhood I once knew? To my right, everything looks as before, but turning to the left in the direction of the bakery, I am confronted with a sight for which there could only be one explanation. The trees, already bereft of their leaves, are stripped of their natural brown bark as well as of most of their branches, some of which stretch plaintively into the acrid air. The smell of sulfur is so strong it burns my throat. Further on it mixes with the sickening smell of burnt flesh. The facades of the houses on the opposite side are riddled with dozens of holes from shrapnel spewed everywhere. Closer to the bakery, I see shreds of clothing and human flesh hanging from trees and, as I scan the whole area around me, balconies across the street are dotted with them as well. The street is deserted; I am the only living being in this valley of death, looking for bread, the staff of life.

Near the bakery, a woman is lying close to the curb - dead - her legs blown off. In my confusion I almost fall over her, then recoil in horror. A few steps away is the bakery - or where it was once - now a gaping hole. Plaintive cries are coming from next door, the first signs of life. Had someone carried the survivors inside the house so quickly? There is no living person in sight. Only moans and muffled cries from inside the house. A shudder runs through me. I flee this scene of death as if pursued by the spirits of the underworld.

Our dark cellar seems a haven to me but when I try to say what I have just seen, nothing coherent comes out of my mouth, only broken fragments of a sentence, "The Stalinorgel... bakery... a dead woman... moans... cries... flesh hanging from trees." I feel someone putting an arm around me and holding something under my nose. It is Frau Kaiser, the doctor's wife. As soon as my breath comes back to me, I have to give a full account of what everyone understands now to have happened to the bakery. When I have come to the end, we hear Fee's voice, the words tumbling out of her mouth with such anguish that we all look at her in open dismay when she tells us, "My mother ... she was waiting in that line for bread." All our attention is now turned to Fee who has grown pale and wide-eyed from fear. My God, I think, it's not possible... it can't be.

We now recall that no one had seen her for the last two hours or more and those standing around Fee volunteer all kinds of suggestions for her disappearance.

"Perhaps she went to another store and is hiding in another shelter," someone suggests.

"Yes, she may have heard the explosion and wants to wait until it is safe to return," another offers this alternative.

Fee, frightened by my report, wants to go look for her mother among the dead and the wounded. We discourage her from doing so and tell her that someone else will go. But who?

"She may have escaped with the retreating SS to seek asylum from the enemy's vengeance," someone ventures this possibility. Fee dismisses it as being very unlike her mother to leave her only child exposed to the wrath of the Russian occupiers. But we argue in return that she could not implicate Fee in her plans to escape without endangering her daughter's safety.

"She probably did not want to tell you her whereabouts in case the Russians interrogate you. It is not easy to hide the truth for long."

Fee, however, still clings to the hope that her mother will return when she thinks it is safe to leave her present shelter, wherever that may be.

She feels strengthened in that hope. We form a circle around Fee who is sitting quietly, not comprehending. She insists that her mother is hiding somewhere. "She will come back. I know she will... when it is safe for her."

She never did.

———

After the Stalinorgel hit, the mood in the cellar turned funereal, even though the shelling had grown less frequent. We no longer trusted the eerie silence between attacks because it spoke a language all its own, louder than the guns of the artillery and the explosion of its bombs. We knew that the battle of Berlin was drawing to a close, but wondered how many more victims it would claim before it had run its course.

Fee meanwhile was remarkably calm, too calm. The only reason for her quiet resignation was that hope still sustained her. She seemed removed from the events around her which had diminished in importance against the vaster prospect of her mother's final disappearance. It was as if her mother already gave her sustenance from the world beyond, to bless her with tranquility and fortitude for the life of an orphan at fifteen.

We looked upon her as an orphan already and attended to her with tactful solicitude, strengthening her for the possibility of a life without her mother. Her tragedy brought her closer to us but also set her apart. She had become another of the bereaved in a war that had left so many orphans or widows. She had become what my father called, "*Ein Kind des Schicksals*," a child of fate.

In the evening of our ninth day below, a group of German soldiers passed through our basement like phantoms from another realm. They looked worn and dirty, tired and disheveled, their weapons slung loosely over their drooping shoulders or held negligently in their hands.

"We are no longer fighting," they told us lethargically. "We are in retreat, trying to stay ahead of the Russians who are everywhere in Berlin. They've surrounded it. We would be grateful if any one of you could supply us with civilian clothes. The Russians will be here tomorrow... there won't be any fighting in this district or anywhere else."

They left as mysteriously as they came after taking a sip of water or a crust of stale bread, leaving us with the reality of having to face the

Russians at dawn. Our only comfort was that our neighborhood would possibly be spared street fighting.

That same evening, during another conference, five or six men appointed my father to be the arbitrator between them and the victorious Russian army. I stood next to him, listening to the discussion and watched how this man, my father, once powerless, humiliated, hounded and harassed for twelve grueling years, had suddenly become the spokesman, the last hope for fair treatment that these people hoped to get from their occupiers. Now they appealed to him to speak on their behalf if questioned about their behavior towards him, the Jew, and his family. He stood among them, taller than most, though not quite as erect as in former days, thinner and grayer from years of physical and psychological hardships, and told them in a quiet, firm voice that he would be a fair and honest witness if called upon to be their judge. I wondered whether they would have done the same for him if the outcome had been different. He qualified his statement by saying that he could only speak for their attitude towards him but that he could not speak for any involvement they may have had in the affairs of the Third Reich, trivial or serious. They came to an agreement, the crowning irony of the whole reversal of our situations. One of them suggested that we put on the yellow star once more to greet the first Russians entering our street.

"They won't do anything to you. And they will believe you more than us when you speak on our behalf."

My father joked about it later in private, "The master race is losing some of its mastery," and my mother added with a wry smile, "History is the supreme trickster, making fools of us all."

We put on the yellow star again with very different feelings than four years before. This badge of former shame, meant for our humiliation and to make us easy targets for abuse, was now to serve as our protection. The Star of David, defaced and ridiculed, would once again come into its legitimate power, reemerging from the ashes of history.

That night, sleep came to few of us. The silence around us was absolute. Our vigilance was at a pitch. Unfamiliar noises, echoing in the thick and muted darkness, stiffened our spines in readiness for encountering the sudden presence of men in strange uniforms, groping their way through unfamiliar pathways. We listened for their heavy boots and the sounds of a foreign tongue. What could we expect from these soldiers in the first flurry of victory, their minds seething with the memories of German arrogance, trampling on their sacred soil and their people? How could we cross the barriers of anger and fear even if some among them spoke our language? I reviewed the few Russian words I had learned from my Ukrainian co-workers and knew they would be woefully inadequate to explain to them the complexities of our situation. How could we have remained alive when so many Jews had not, they would want to know.

My family talked throughout the night without making any concrete plans, mindful of the fact that they might fail. The concept of being given a future was still strange to us and we approached it tentatively, prefacing our remarks with *falls*, in case. We wondered what the chances were for building a life in this devastated graveyard of a city. My parents liked to remember another Berlin, the Berlin of their youth, when its pulse was beating with the vitality and excitement of a city in bloom, when it was a trend-setting, cultural center that attracted people from all corners of the world, when it looked at its Jewish citizens as the architects of its golden days. I had fallen in love with tales of that Berlin and grieved for its demise.

The night was slowly edging its way towards morning and we went from the past to the present. With the coming of the Russians we again feared the collapse of civilized behavior; again feared that morality and respect for human dignity would be thrown into the trashcan of history.

And yet our imagination did not, nor dared not, stretch beyond the limits set by human decency.

Soon after dawn on May 4th, our air-raid warden approached my father with a suggestion. "Perhaps you should go outside now to investigate the situation and 'welcome' the first Russians."

My father, Hans, and I put on our yellow stars and slowly climbed down the stairs to the street, confident that the Russians would know this sign on our coats and greet us as our liberators from a common enemy. We were listening for voices, boots, the clatter of tanks, but there was no sound anywhere except that of our own footsteps.

The air was heavy with expectation.

The barricade across the street blocked our view to the left; to the right of us, the street was devoid of life and of color. The sky above us cast a melancholy face on all the familiar objects and drenched them with a damp cold that went through our coats and our hearts. As we climbed on top of the barricade, the sense of deathly lassitude grew even stronger and spoke to me of betrayal, sadness, and the enormous futility the war had left as a memento. The violence done to this small strip of earth felt like the violence done to a human being. The wounds lay open as silent witnesses to human insanity.

The SS building across the street, empty now of its dreaded content and riddled with holes from flying shrapnel, still had the power to evoke fear in me as I remembered the many times when I, with my yellow star in full view, had to pass the guard standing in front of it. The grim echoes of arrogant voices seemed to roam through the deserted rooms of the spectral building while we waited for the sound of Russian voices.

We did not have to wait long.

Looking to the end of the street to our left we saw two figures turning the corner into our street. They were wearing grey-green uniforms and were lightly armed. "Russians," we said in unison. Both men were still young, one taller than the other and in his early twenties, the other shorter and no more than sixteen. They spied us on the barricade and walked towards us with leisurely steps, smiling in response to our tentative gestures of greeting. Then they stood next to us so quickly as if sprung from the earth.

"*Guten Tag*," the older one addressed us with the familiar greeting in German, meaning, no doubt, to reassure us that he meant no harm. He looked at our yellow stars and his expression changed from bemusement to perplexity. He was blond and blue-eyed, his features clean-shaven and handsome, with a natural gentleness about them that made me trust him in an instant. Pointing his index finger at our yellow stars, he shook his head. He doesn't believe we are Jews, the thought pierced me. He tried to explain himself in broken German, "*Hitler macht Juden kaputt*," and emphasized his meaning with a gesture that indicated decapitation. He proved it by telling us that he saw some Jews here in Berlin hanging from trees. He could not believe that any Jews had survived the mass killings he had seen in his battles throughout Eastern Europe.

More with gestures than with words we tried to convince him that a handful of other Jews had survived. We showed him our papers with the "J" still imprinted on them and our signatures of "Israel" and "Sara." Still, he shook his head. We grew desperate. Again with gestures and few words we told him of our life under the Nazis. He listened with interest, his face taking on a more thoughtful expression. All of a sudden his eyes lit up with an idea and he asked us, "*Sag das Sh'ma*." We smiled with relief, each one of us saying the *Sh'ma* as though we were in our synagogue again. He heaved a sigh of relief and shook our hands as though he had found a long-lost friend. He told us his name was Sasha. "*Hitler schlecht...*" he confided freely, "*sehr schlecht... aber jetzt kaputt. Gut... sehr gut...*"

He explained why he had hesitated for so long to believe that we were Jews. Russian troops had come upon concentration camps that confronted them with so great a human calamity that many of the soldiers sickened at the sight of the emaciated, abused, and helpless prisoners, many of them near death or madness. Among these miserable victims were many who looked suspiciously well-fed and strong. The Russian liberators soon discovered that these men were impostors, masquerading as Jews to hide their former identities as SS men. When word got out that this was happening in several camps, the soldiers were instructed to adopt a foolproof method of exposing the pretenders. Reciting the whole Jewish creed, the *Sh'ma*, in Hebrew would surely be a test only Jews could pass. And they were right. Those suspected to be SS men fell into their trap and met their punishment, either on the spot or in Siberia.

Sasha's account, in limited German, required too abstract a conceptualization in my mind to evoke the pictures of concentration camps that I would later see in print; yet his mention of the contrast between the inmates and the SS guards confirmed a truth we had all along suspected. Our response to what the Allied liberators found in the death traps of Germany and elsewhere was a silent shaking of heads. Impossible to comprehend. What abject cowardice, what confounded hypocrisy came to the light of day for these pretenders to vaulting superiority when coming face to face with their own demise. And I remembered Frau Burger. She too had tried to save her skin through an eleventh-hour attempt to find refuge in the space occupied by a Jewish family whose presence she had thought earlier would contaminate her.

The pain of remembrance must have shown in my face for Sasha suddenly turned knight errant when he offered me his protection against possible dangers from his fellow comrades.

"*Du... schönes Fräulein,*" I heard him say, pointing his finger at me, "*Ruski Soldat hat gern schöne Fräulein,*" You are a beautiful young girl... Russian soldiers like beautiful girls." Despite his compliment, I must have turned pale because he was quick to assure me that as far as his power would extend, he would not let men, starved for women, lay hands on me. He could, he added with regret, only exert his authority as a sergeant with men of his regiment. He suggested I keep wearing the yellow star and let it work in my favor.

There was a difference between the Russian fighting forces and those who would eventually occupy Berlin. It seemed we had little to fear from the troops engaged in fighting those small pockets of German resistance still fighting for their Führer. The occupying forces, however, might not deal so charitably with Berliners.

Sasha the man presented a phenomenon to me: how a human being could so staunchly cling to his integrity, his humanity under such crushing circumstances as he had experienced. Perhaps because he had looked into the abyss of human depravity, he wanted to distance himself from it.

We returned to the cellar where everyone had been anxious about our long absence. Together with the other tenants we waited out the arrival of more troops.

The sound of rattling tanks on our street shook us into awareness that a confrontation with our occupiers was imminent. My father, Hans, and I went upstairs in the company of our warden who was going to be the spokesperson for the entire apartment building. I felt we had nothing to fear from our liberators as long as the yellow star spoke for us.

How futile the raising of the barricade had been against the assault of massive Russian tanks was evident as soon as we stepped out into the street. The barricade had fallen like a house of cards. The street bore the deep imprints of tanks having passed already on their way through the city. Two tanks, carrying Russian soldiers, had stopped in front of our house. Residents from neighboring houses were flocking around them with vague smiles on faces that had a guarded look, part welcome and part apprehension. The soldiers responded by throwing them pieces of bread and waving to children. It was an astounding sight. I hold this picture of compassion fast in my heart. What must we have looked like to them who had seen unimaginable scenes of human suffering, whether from starvation, disease, or wounds inflicted by weapons of war?

One of the men, an officer to judge by the insignia on his uniform and air of authority, stepped down from his tank and, focusing his eyes on my father, walked towards him with purposeful steps. I went cold with fright. He asked my father, "*Wo ist Funkturm?*" Where is the radio tower? "*Komm!*" He beckoned my father to follow him. I watched with mounting dread and as I saw my father climb onto the tank my vision blurred and I cried out in terror, "No, Papa... don't go." The memory of another moment in time had me see in the tank a truck loaded with SS men, now come to take my father away forever. The officer sensed my panic and told me in broken German that my father would return after he had taken them to the radio tower.

My fear soon turned to pride when I saw my father wave to me from the tank with a smile. Whatever they wanted him to do, I saw him endowed with a new energy, a new dignity as he assumed his responsibility to assist our liberators, a dignity that should have been his all along.

A few months later, after order had been partially restored, we learned what the Russians had found in the bunker of the Reichskanzlei. Hitler was dead in his bunker. All of them -- Hitler, his wife of a few days, and the Goebbels family -- had taken the easy way out by suicide.

Ashes and carnage -- the legacy left by the fabricators of the Thousand Year Reich -- how merciful a death for them. How cruel a one for their victims.

One day, with the pretext of taking a census, the occupying Russian commander issued an order for all tenants of our apartment building to gather in one room. For all of my seventeen years, I was unable to form a clear picture in my mind of what it would be like to stand face to face with a reputed rapist. I recalled the panic I felt on seeing the giant web of tracks in the railroad yard, imagining being run over by a locomotive. That was how a rapist, with gun in hand, appeared to me then.

The tenants of Sybelstrasse 62 gathered in the apartment of Herr Hoigt on the ground floor.

"It's a trap," someone suggested.

"It's a ruse to look for women," another was more outspoken.

"Make yourselves look ugly," was the advice given to women.

The whole house was on the alert, no one felt safe from the avenging victors.

Upstairs in our apartment, Lydia helped Felizitas and me "disguise" ourselves. She put dark scarves on our heads that hid all of our hair and part of our faces. She put a thin layer of white powder on our cheeks and dark shadows under our eyes to make us look sickly. As to her own person, she decked herself out as though she were expecting her favorite lover. "I don't care what happens to me..." she explained, "but you two..."

We joined the tenants already gathered in Herr Hoigt's room. My mother, Felizitas and I chose a corner of the room furthest away from the entrance while my father and brother placed themselves in front of us.

Our eyes were fastened on the door to watch for our supposed census takers, a story I very much wanted to believe. No one in the room spoke. Everyone sat huddled in their winter coats, the women wearing our scarves as if we were hiding behind a fortress.

Suddenly the door opened with a sweeping motion and three uni-
formed officers entered the room with imperious steps. It did not take
us long to realize that they were no census takers, for they hardly glanced
at the men and, with hawk-like eyes, searched the room for female prey.
They seemed to have found what they were looking for as they took rapid
steps towards Felizitas and me. But Lydia, getting up from her chair, in-
tercepted them midway, placed herself in front of them, smiled and waved
her index finger, saying one word they knew well, "*Komm!*" All three of
them, taken in by her most captivating, professional smile and her good
looks, looked at her with appreciation and followed her out the door like
bees after honeysuckle.

Oh my God, I thought, all three of them. Even though men had been
her business, these officers will not see the woman in her but an object
of their starved lust and revenge. Lydia, who had shared her bed with SS
men, had become the guardian angel of a Jewish girl. Let history be her
judge.

Not long after my narrow escape from becoming another nameless sta-
tistic in the long list of women raped or killed by men dizzy with victory,
Sasha, on being told about the incident with the three officers, unleashed
his fury in a string of Russian invectives that more than anything per-
suaded me of the sincerity in his efforts to keep me from harm. I heard in
his voice the genuine cry of indignation. The fact that these three soldiers
may have been of higher rank only added to his anger since they were
bound by a code of honor to refrain from raping and looting. His suggestion, therefore, that I take refuge for a while in the apartment of a house
that a group of Russian officers had chosen as their temporary headquarters struck me as odd after what I had just told him. These officers, he assured my parents, would not violate the Geneva treaty agreements. Sasha
took me to the house where my mother's family had their store and living
quarters. I drew some comfort from that.

We entered a room filled with smoke and the deep hum of male voices. Sasha, conferring with one of the officers, clad in his starched uniform studded with medals, looking well-fed and smoking a cigar, pointed in my direction.

Hush fell momentarily over the room. I felt my muscles tense involuntarily as all eyes scanned me from head to toe, then rested on my yellow star. I was standing in the doorway, not at all sure whether I wanted to enter this den of hungry wolves. Would they see the German in me rather than the Jew? Would their code of honor hold up under the urgency of their natural impulses?

Sasha, watching my hesitation, came up to me. He put his hand on my arm and introduced me to the officer in charge who, in turn, pointed to a corner of the room where I could seat myself.

When I felt sure they were tending to their own affairs once more and did not with so much as a glance acknowledge my presence, I looked for routes of escape just in case it might become necessary. After more than an hour in this tangle of male bodies and the biting smell of tobacco, I got up with the pretext that I wanted to find a bathroom. I had truly become non-existent for them, so I made my way to the front entrance and, looking to see whether any one was watching me, slipped out into the street. It was that easy.

The cool air returned my equilibrium.

Sasha was a true friend. He understood my reluctance to stay alone in the apartment with men who had not been in the company of women for many weeks or months on end. On one of his visits he came with sad news. He had been called to fight a pocket of German soldiers who remained true to Hitler's desperate last orders to defend Berlin to the last drop of German blood.

"War not finished..." Sasha said matter-of-factly. "But soon... *Deutschland kaputt*." There was both determination and weariness in his tone, and I felt more than ever the insanity of a war that might claim the lives of the best of human beings like Sasha.

His departure was like the going out of a bright candle in a dark room.

My family was sitting around the dining room table in a state of tension. None of us was under the illusion that all of our Russian occupiers would respect the yellow star if their instincts dictated otherwise. After discussing possible options of how to evade their grip, it was decided that only my father should answer the doorbell with "Nix" to their demands for "*Frau.*"

We did not have to wait long to put our plan into action. One afternoon there was a loud, peremptory knocking at the front door. My father, as planned, went to open it and within a matter of seconds returned with two drunken soldiers trailing behind him. One of them grinned sheepishly as he tottered toward me and said the only two German words he had learned, "*Komm, Frau.*" I shook my head and pointed to the yellow star on my left, telling him, "*Ya yevreika.*" His grin widened, "*Ya tozhe yevrei,*" (I'm Jewish too). If this was meant to be an invitation, I had no inclination to follow it.

He was moving closer to me and, expecting that he would use force, my mother stepped between us, yelling a firm "No" and, saying in turn her "*Komm,*" she led him to the back bedroom. His companion stayed behind, looking sheepishly at us and, on much more steady feet, guarded us all the while.

My mother returned with the drunken soldier after a short time, much too short for him to have carried out the business for which he came. He barked a short order to his companion and they both left in a hasty retreat.

"He tried," my mother laughed, "but the vodka wouldn't let him." The thought that my angelic mother would have had to submit to his brute touch was to me more like blasphemy than a sacrifice.

After that, we decided on a strategy for the safety of both my mother and myself. I was going to hide in a small storage area above the bathroom while my mother would leave by the back staircase from the kitchen to hide in her sister's store. My brother had to stay home to help with the ladder while my father would answer the front door.

It was early one afternoon when there was another loud, familiar rapping on the front door. We all jumped into position. My mother hurried to the back stairs, my brother held the stepladder for me to climb into my new hiding place, and my father walked slowly to the entrance hall to open the door. A second, more impatient pounding announced the urgency of the visitors' purpose.

From my hiding place, I could just barely hear the hoarse demand for "Frau" and imagined my father shaking his head and saying "Nix" when I heard a shot. Then silence; total, torturous silence.

My first impulse was to rush from my spot to see whether my father was all right but I checked myself in time. I could not let them know of my presence after my father told them, "Nix Frau." I had to wait. I felt like someone bound and gagged.

Still numb with fright, I opened the door of my hiding place slightly after what seemed like a lifetime. I was met with only silence. But then I heard the front door open and footsteps coming in my direction. "*Püppchen?*" my father called quietly.

"Papa," I screamed and almost jumped from my perch into his arms. Trailing behind him were two pale-faced figures: my mother and Hans.

We gathered in the dining room and my father, seething with rage, paced the floor while he told us what had happened, how one of the two Russians had taken his pistol and aimed it at my father when he answered with "Nix" to his demand for "*Frau.*" Too drunk to hit my father, the bullet hit the ceiling above his head instead. Both my father and brother ran down the stairs as fast as their shaking knees would carry them.

"I've had enough!" my father shouted at some invisible adversary. "First Hitler and now these..." He stormed out of the apartment like an angry god.

Not long after he had left, he reentered our living room in high spirits, waving a piece of paper in his hand. On it was written in beautiful Russian orthography, "This is a Jewish family who suffered persecution under Hitler and is not to be molested under penalty of death." It was signed by a major Kalinsky.

It looked like a love poem to me.

Chapter 7

Passages

Omnia mutantur;
omnia fluunt
—OVID, *Metamorphoses*

One piece of evidence from the early days of 1948, a small date book, is still in my possession. I am struck by seeing that I dressed the German words of my daily entries in Hebrew letters. I had no secrets to hide from anyone who chanced to come upon this little book. I had no confessions to make of my inner life, like Anne Frank did with her "Dear Kitty." No doubt the code I chose for my record keeping expressed the need for the true identity that I had long been denied. Having recently turned twenty, I wanted to reclaim my life as my own, not governed by external forces, but following instead a voice from within. That voice told me that henceforth it was up to me to salvage from the past what would best shape my future in compliance with my natural inclinations, my untapped potential. The Hebrew alphabet linked the past to the future. It was my memorial to the dead and my commitment to the living.

———

Berlin in 1948 was a city where dreams died quickly under the harsh necessities of daily existence. The German need for *Kultur*, nevertheless, asserted itself with remarkable energy. My friend Ruth and I rushed into the world of sound and song welcoming us from the stage of the newly renovated *Opernhaus* and the *Schiller Theater*. The German language was made melodious to us again by the great actors of the theater. We learned that it could and did aspire to lofty heights when it extolled the humanistic ideals of tolerance and justice, as in Lessing's *Nathan der Weise*, Goethe's *Iphigenia*, or Schiller's *Don Carlos*. The stage became the mirror in which we saw reflected the human capacity for good or evil and, just as we had rejoiced when the allied forces triumphed over the Nazi menace, so we now relished the defeat of the villain at the end of a play. We learned that Evil is ubiquitous, that Shakespeare's assessment, "Humanity must perforce prey on itself, like monsters of the deep," is a universal truth.

The journal entries, beginning January 1 and ending May 26, my last day in Berlin, show those days as being divided between the present and the future. The present was essentially a prelude to the future, a waiting time for our exit permits to be able to realize our dream of starting a new life in America. There were early signs that my mother's x-ray, still showing traces of her earlier TB, would prevent her from getting an exit permit. A doctor of the American Consulate assured us that providing her with sufficient care would eventually allow her to recover enough to emigrate. That hope grew in me to a promise. I decided to leave Germany alone in preparation for my family coming later, when I could then be their guide in making a new home in America.

One day in April, my emigration papers finally looked promising. The earliest date the Consulate gave me for emigrating was May. The conflict it provoked in me was profound. I literally trembled with elation and misgivings. I derived comfort from a coincidence: Ruth and her family were scheduled to leave the same day, June 15, 1948.

I left Berlin on May 26 to go to Bremerhaven, where I waited to board the ship to America. Leaving my family had been wrenching; between my father's endless censures of my wanting to leave the family now of my own free will after the Nazis had failed to separate us by force, and my mother's quiet encouragement to find my own path, I felt tossed from one to the other, from being a dutiful daughter to becoming a free agent and building my life. My selfishness was apparent to me but, like birds who must leave their nests, I too had to spread my wings for a second birth. I cushioned the pain of separation by clinging to the image of an eventual reunion.

When I waved farewell to my family from the train that was to take me to Bremerhaven, the tears running down my cheeks distorted the sight of them as though I was looking at a mirage.

I was grateful to be in the company of Ruth and her family, but missed my own family all the more, tormented by an insistent question: Had I made the right decision? Will regrets come stalking me in time?

At long last we embarked on the "Marine Flasher," an old trunk of a ship that had been used to transport American soldiers during the war. The irony of using the same ship that had sent our liberators to us and that was going to send us now to their land did not pass without comment among us. Though it looked more like a galley to transport prisoners, to us it felt safe and throbbing with expectations.

On a day after having seen nothing but ocean water for a week, Ruth and I were asleep on the lower deck with other passengers when we were awakened by shouts of "Get up! Hurry! We see her...." Half awake and feeling disoriented, I scrambled down from the upper bunk of the bed I shared with Ruth and, as though someone had called "Fire!" we rushed upstairs to see what all the excitement was about. It was the hour of the morning when the world greets us with half-closed eyes, not yet ready to admit the rays of the rising sun. It took me some time to make out the dim shades of land that rose across the brooding darkness over the water. And then we saw her, "in the dawn's early light," the proud Lady of Liberty, welcoming us as she had welcomed so many millions before to the safety of her shores. My heart was beating in my throat, choked with gratitude and wonder; I could not tell whether it was tears or the morning dew that wet my cheeks, when I felt a hand being firmly planted on my shoulder.

We were all looking straight ahead at this colossal promise of "Liberty and Justice for all." There was nothing for us to say at this solemn and humbling moment. Our future beckoned to us, promising that once we touched solid land, it would be ours to grasp.

The Silberberg family was going to leave for Kansas City, where friends of Ruth's father were expecting their arrival. I was left in the care of HIAS, in a city with a tangle of contradictions to me. New York was strangely exhilarating one moment and frightening the next; at times challenging, at times intimidating. Walking in a crowd of people rushing about their daily business made me feel vibrantly alive; walking beneath those towering skyscrapers cut off my breath. I felt small and lost, wedged between immensely tall giants of steel and cement whose tops seemed to lean conspiratorially toward each other, ready to crush me. I became the little girl in the stroller again, going through the dark and narrow tunnel, only this time there was no maternal voice telling me, "It's all right, *Püppchen*." How could people ever get used to living in this quarry of a city, so inimical to human warmth and the living breath of nature?

And then there were the police sirens. The first time I heard one go off, I followed an old reflex and turned to look for the nearest air-raid shelter, until I noticed that people kept on walking, seemingly oblivious to this cutting sound. The whirring of planes overhead were reminders of the bombers that had turned my insides to ice.

However much I wanted to run from the past, it came rushing back in unexpected ways. I was more than a foreigner, more than a greenhorn, I was a reincarnation from another era. The ostentatious flaunting of wealth and abundance around me made me all the more aware of my own penury and exclusion in the land of plenty. I indulged in the most avaricious fantasies. I wanted it all, this pair of red shoes, that blouse with the lace collar, and that skirt with the full flounce.

With the few dollars I managed to save from the meager allowance given to us by HIAS, I bought myself the coveted pair of red shoes. In an instant, New York became a friendlier place, though it offered no allure for me to stay longer than was necessary. My friend Vera, who had survived Auschwitz and rung my doorbell in Sybelstrasse soon after Liberation, urged me to come and live in Boston, a city reminiscent of Berlin. I was more than ready, eager to leave my host city New York, so indifferent to timid souls.

My stay in Vera's small apartment was short-lived. Our disparate experiences during the war had altered our temperaments to such an extent that we started quarreling over trivial matters like which color lipstick to use. Our differences finally became as sharp as a razor and I left my jailor to become an *au pair* girl for a Jewish family with two children in Needham, Massachusetts. I spent some happy months there, supported and encouraged in all the attempts I made to realize dreams held captive for years by jealous gods. My first step into the world of learning and ideas came with my acceptance at Simmons College for girls, fertile soil for a novice like me in Academia.

There was only one blight in this period of growth. A phone call from my father gave me the bitter news that my mother, after finally receiving her exit permit, had been diagnosed with Parkinson's Disease. I was never to welcome her in my new home. She remained an invalid for the next eight years, until her death in 1958. I visited her for the first and last time in the summer of 1954 with my two-year old son, Kenneth. Remorse and grief were to be my companions for years to come. This country of strangers felt too vast for my comprehension. I stood like a beggar outside the mansion of a rich lord, an exile, feeling cold and abandoned. I turned to what was closest at hand. There were my books, my classes, my assignments, some new friends, and the concentrated effort of making a new language my own. My tongue did acrobatics as I tried to cleanse my pronunciation of the harsher German gutturals.

I spent more time listening to others talking than speaking of my own accord.

I became a parrot in order to hide my fear of making mistakes.

I listened to soap operas on the radio in order to familiarize myself with the vernacular.

I smiled when others laughed at jokes or made puns I did not understand.

Finally I developed symptoms of having difficulty swallowing. Gradually, in the presence of Dr. Wolf, a psychiatrist, I started to lift the lid off the Pandora's box that I had carried with me unknowingly across the ocean.

The complete opening of the box occurred over a span of many years; years of marriage, of raising children, of studying, of teaching.

Only then was I able to release its contents into the full light of consciousness.

Only then could I name the demons and recount their deeds both in public speaking and in writing.

Breaking the silence was my second liberation.

Berkeley, California, 1992. From being a survivor of one of the most turbulent and bloody periods in human history, I have become an ordinary woman, full of memories clinging to my very soul.

I look back on a life filled with joy and with sorrow, with success and with failure, and, above all, with tasks not yet accomplished.

There was once a marriage of fourteen years that ended in divorce when the youngest of our four children was only three months old.

There was my dream of pursuing an education which I realized when I received my Ph.D. in Comparative Literature from the University of California at Berkeley while, at the same time, raising our four children. My children know my story and have entered a world of diversity as compassionate and understanding human beings. We are close, though miles may separate some of us.

There is still the anguish of the seventeen-year old who wanted to know why she escaped the Nazi conflagration.

There are the faces of the dead who need to be remembered so that their tortured souls will find a resting place in our hearts.

I knew, from 1985 on, that I could no longer remain silent about the twelve years I lived in Hitler's Berlin. I had to join those voices who warn of the dangers of extreme nationalism and racial persecution. My voice would be a small one but, together with others, past injustices would be kept alive by the act of remembrance. The voices may thus serve as guides to warn against repetitions of state-sponsored genocide and the violation of human rights and dignity.

Since the mid-nineteen eighties I have spoken to hundreds of young people in schools and wherever I have been invited to tell my survival story. Their eloquent responses bolstered my resolve to teach about the failure of speaking out when any group is a target for hatred because of race, gender, or belief. The courage to protest, as was shown in Rosenstrasse in 1943, must always be called upon to help save human lives from the hands of murderers.

Telling the survival story in public inevitably brings a host of questions with it. Is it possible at all to do justice to this vastly complex phenomenon of the six million Jews and leave the listeners with the appropriate repugnance and indignation at this outbreak of human barbarity? Can we, who escaped the ultimate fate of the victims of the Final Solution, give adequate testimony to their sufferings? Those voices could tell us of the last hours of their death by gas, or by being buried alive, or by the knife of Dr. Mengele; those voices have been silenced forever. We cannot penetrate that silence to look into their souls. All that is left is to record the mundane yet horrific circumstances of their untimely deaths.

Mira, my closest friend from 1939-1943 -- what would she say to my attempts to speak the unspeakable? I would not presume to speak of her suffering, of her multiple epileptic seizures in the collection center in Grosse Hamburgerstrasse, nor of her ordeal in the cattle car, nor of her entrance through the gates of Auschwitz where her life ended at fifteen. All I can do is to speak of what it was like to have been born a Jew in Hitler's Germany.

And how dare we who lived through those deadly times, how dare we interrupt the dance of present life to hold up, as it were, this monstrous face of the past, of our human nature? Are we not ghouls, golems, spectres come from another world?

Another world? It has been and still is our world. The nightmare from which those survivors awakened has not ended for all people. Human cruelty, we see, has no national boundaries, no one skin color, no particular culture. The builders of the Third Reich have engendered their copy cats.

The Shoah stands unique in the annals of human atrocities, planned and supported by some of the best minds in Europe. The good is too often overpowered by the agents of evil who grow in our midst before we find ways to nip that growth in the bud. All of us, at different times, have not yet learned to tame the demons within us instead of projecting them onto our perceived adversaries.

So, why speak at all?

Because we must – we must speak for the dead or they will die a second death, leaving no trace in the annals of history where they have their rightful space, just as we still recite ritually the hardships of the Israelites under the "Pharaoh who did not know Joseph" (Exodus 1:8).

We must speak in the hope of appealing to the good impulses of the human heart that will, in the end, supplant the evil; in the hope of building a more humane and equitable fellowship among all nations.

The well-worn saying, "In Remembrance Lies Salvation," must still be our motto, our guide for action.

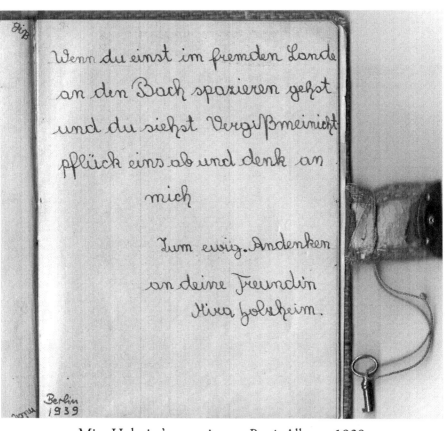

Mira Holzeim's entry in my *Poesie* Album, 1939

If ever in a foreign land
you walk beside a brook
and you see forget-me-nots,
pick one and think of me.

In everlasting memory,
Your friend,
Mira Holzheim. 1939

Acknowledgments

This memoir had a long gestation period before it reached the desks of Barany Consulting. My deep appreciation belongs to Beth Barany, my writing coach, and her husband Ezra Barany who was in charge of production.

Their enthusiasm, sense of purpose, and thoughtfulness was a sustaining comfort to my sometimes flagging spirits.

To my family belongs my gratitude for voluntarily taking on the task of editing: to my daughters, Rachel, Sarah and Ruth, and to Daniel, Nancy and Bob. They travelled back with me into a world where evil overpowered goodness. My four children, bless them, have been my stalwart companions through laughter and through tears for these many years.

Alison Owings, author of "Frauen: German Women Recall the Third Reich," interviewed me for her book, and has ever since been a devoted friend and a supporter of my creative ventures. I cherish and feel enriched by her loyalty and occasional lapses into German.

Last, but not least indeed, I am beholden to friends and members of my immediate community for their lively interest in my memoir, too many to list by name. They encouraged me to come out of hiding so that the world could know my story of survival, it being also their story.

About the Author

Rita Jenny Kuhn was born on November 29, 1927 in Berlin, Germany, of Jewish parents, Fritz and Frieda Kuhn.

Determined to complete her education, she emigrated to America after the war in 1948. Rita married in 1951 and had four children. She received her Master's degree in Classics at Cornell University in 1963.

After her divorce in 1965, Rita raised her four children as a single mother, while also attending graduate school and receiving her Doctorate in Comparative Literature at the University of California, Berkeley in 1984. She also spent twelve years as a tutor for disadvantaged children at Berkeley High School.

Since 1985, she has shared her story of survival with high school students throughout the San Francisco Bay Area. Rita is the proud grandmother of five grandchildren and lives in Berkeley, California.

Made in the USA
Lexington, KY
09 March 2013